Partnership with the Dying

Where Medicine and Ministry Should Meet

David H. Smith

ROWMAN & LITTLEFIELD PUBLISHERS, INC.
Lanham • Boulder • New York • Toronto • Oxford

ROWMAN & LITTLEFIELD PUBLISHERS, INC.

Published in the United States of America
by Rowman & Littlefield Publishers, Inc.
A wholly owned subsidiary of The Rowman & Littlefield Publishing Group, Inc.
4501 Forbes Boulevard, Suite 200, Lanham, Maryland 20706
www.rowmanlittlefield.com

PO Box 317
Oxford
OX2 9RU, UK

British Library Cataloguing in Publication Information Available

Library of Congress Cataloging-in-Publication Data

Smith, David H., 1939–
    Partnership with the dying : where medicine and ministry should meet / David H.
Smith.
        p. cm.
    Includes bibliographical references and index.
    ISBN 0-7425-4466-4 (hardcover : alk. paper) — ISBN 0-7425-4467-2 (pbk. :
alk. paper)
    1. Church work with the terminally ill—United States. 2. Terminal care—
Religious aspects—Christianity. 3. Death—Religious aspects—Christianity.
I. Title.

    BV4460.6.S65 2005
    259'.4175—dc22

                                                                    2004023615

Printed in the United States of America

⊗™ The paper used in this publication meets the minimum requirements of
American National Standard for Information Sciences—Permanence of Paper
for Printed Library Materials, ANSI/NISO Z39.48-1992.

For
Daniel L. Arnaud,
Hugh C. Laughlin[+],
Albert Wertheim

~

Contents

	Preface	ix
Chapter 1	Introduction and Method	1
Chapter 2	Conversation Partners	15
Chapter 3	Explaining and Justifying	39
Chapter 4	Deciding for Death	63
Chapter 5	Community and Compromise	83
Chapter 6	Conclusion	107
	Appendix	123
	Index	131
	About the Author	135

~

Preface

This book has been more than six years in the making—a long pregnancy for a short volume. In the course of its gestation I have accumulated many debts. The first is to The Lilly Endowment, Inc., which funded the research on which the book is based. Lilly's grant has already led to the production of two books—one I edited called *Caring Well: Religion, Narrative, and Health Care Ethics* and Richard Miller's *Children, Ethics, and Modern Medicine*. This volume marks the completion of the endeavor. The work has been a joy for all scholars involved, and I know I speak for all when I express thanks for the Endowment's generous grant support.

But that is just the beginning. Judith Granbois, then Program Associate at the Poynter Center at Indiana University, did about half the interviewing, made more constructive suggestions, and endured more indecisiveness and authorial uncertainty than I can calculate. Judy is a better interviewer than I, and her dedication to this project was inspiring. Early in the planning process, we assembled a small advisory committee consisting of Sandra DeWeese, RN; Margaret Gaffney, MD;

Jennifer Girod, RN, PhD; Kevin McDonnell, PhD; the Reverend Stanley Mullin, PhD; the Reverend Joseph Rautenberg, PhD; and Gail Vance, MD. These friends offered enormous help in identifying persons we might interview, helped us formulate the questions we would ask, and offered occasional critiques of drafts.

Studying transcripts, I discovered, is time-consuming and more difficult than I had supposed. I needed help. That came from Ms. Granbois and from Morna Brothers, Catherine Matthews, and Summer Johnson—younger colleagues who were remarkably insightful. More recently Glenda Murray, who replaced Ms. Granbois on the Center staff, has worked with (and on) me to shape and improve chapters, and to bring the entire project to completion. The manuscript was finished during a year I spent at Yale University with support from its Bioethics Project's Donaghue Initiative. A fine faculty seminar on the lives of professional caregivers was of enormous help—and encouragement. Moreover, fifty students at Yale plowed through an earlier version of the first four chapters in Spring 2004, and their willingness to take it—and our entire seminar—with grace and seriousness is a piece of good fortune I shall never forget. One of those remarkably able students, Sarah Post, was an invaluable reader, critic, and colleague in the final revision.

I hope my respect for and gratitude to the professionals we interviewed comes through on every page of the text. They are remarkable people to whom it was a privilege to listen.

The book is dedicated to the memory of three beloved contemporaries and friends—a rector, brother-in-law, and colleague—who died while the work was in progress. My life has been forever enriched by their humor, courage, friendship, and insight. I hope some of that comes through in the prose, for they are with me "'til the close of the age."

CHAPTER ONE

Introduction and Method

This book addresses two distinguishable but related problems. The first is that dying in America is more difficult than it needs to be. The second is the failure of American Christianity to address the question of care for the dying.

Many Americans are dying bad deaths. More and more people die of old age or chronic illness in hospitals or nursing homes, so that dying has been moved outside the worlds of home and family. In a Western industrialized democracy, death is no longer just a natural process but a technological event that occurs when aggressive medical treatment is stopped. Serious illness, trauma, and dying are facts beyond human control, but we can influence the timing and circumstances of death. Too many health care providers and ordinary citizens continue to regard death as an enemy to be confronted and overcome at any cost, rather than the inevitable fate of all. These facts are not news to anyone who has seriously observed American health care in the last decades, but they reflect a serious problem.

In 1997, American Health Decisions, with funding from the Robert Wood Johnson Foundation, conducted an extensive series of focus groups to explore Americans' values, opinions, and attitudes regarding end-of-life care. They identified a series of "key messages":

- Fear of dying while hooked up to machines instead of dying a natural death in familiar surroundings with their loved ones
- Belief that the current health care system fails to support their concept of an ideal death
- Discomfort with the topic of death and dying and reluctance to take action in advance planning
- Primacy of family considerations in end-of-life decision making
- Failure of current planning options to support their management of death and dying.[1]

It is obvious that these issues could be addressed in religious communities and that those communities—congregations, judicatories, and theological seminaries—are an insufficiently utilized resource in the effort to enable people to live with dying. Religious institutions claim to offer a vision of human life and destiny that places death in perspective, and they constitute communities that can offer communal support for people at the end of their lives. But patients, families, and professionals often fail to tap religious resources for love and support.

Religious communities have not seriously taken up the problems of care for the dying despite incentives provided by several foundations.[2] They have failed to assist with a problem they are expected to know something about. Their absence from the list of key players means that lower-quality care is provided for the dying. Because they have not grappled with the issues as they should, crucial substance is lost from the intellectual and social life of the church. Denial of death within religious communities renders the intellectual and communal claims of those communities disingenuous and incredible. Vital religion must deal honestly and helpfully with death, if it is to have any integrity at all.

The situation is ironic. Every congregation includes members, and clergy, who will tell stories of prolonged or painful deaths of family members. Indeed, widespread recognition that "there's a problem" may be characteristic of congregations. But this generalized interest has not been translated into action within and by religious communities.

Two things are needed if we are to move from this state of generalized awareness to vital connection of religious communities with the problems of care for the dying. The first concerns the religious communities of the United States. Members of congregations must come to see that their traditions say something pertinent, distinctive, and helpful about death and dying. They should have higher expectations that their leaders will inform and lead them in discussion of these matters. They should seek out their members who are nurses, physicians, chaplains, and social workers so as to learn from their experience. Second, health professionals—whether members of congregations or not—should recognize the connection between religion and care for the dying so that they can facilitate discussion, understanding, and effective pastoral care among their professional colleagues.

Health professionals with ties to congregations are a particularly important group, as they have leadership opportunities—and responsibilities—in two walks of life. On the one hand, they can bring their appreciation for the religious or spiritual aspects of care for the dying to the workplace. This insight should lead to an understanding of the religious or spiritual issues that patients or fellow professionals may raise. On the other hand, they are in a position to play a key leadership role within the religious communities of which they are a part.

The religious convictions and judgments of health care professionals have not always been central in recent discussion of care for the dying, and there is a good reason for that caution. A key moral insight at the core of the bioethics movement has concerned professional dominance and patient autonomy. Respect for patient convictions, preferences, and choices should have pride of place over physician (or other professional) paternalism. Robert M. Veatch, one of the best informed and most reliable writers on bioethics for over a third of a century, put it well in his article "Generalization of Expertise."[3] Moral reasoning, Veatch argued, includes a major value premise and a minor factual premise. Professionals might be experts on the factual components of a moral syllogism (e.g., Mr. Smith is having a heart attack) but not on the value components (e.g., all patients having heart attacks should be resuscitated). When professionals claimed expertise in values, they "generalized" their expertise. Patients themselves, rather than medical professionals, should be treated as the experts on the value premises that determine their courses of treatment.

This argument gets at something profoundly right, and it has had the effect of empowering nonphysician moralists who could claim to bring their own distinctive expertise to the debate on care for the dying. But the de-centering of physicians (and nurses, chaplains, and social workers) comes at too high a price if it means not only an end to professional dominance but failure to consider the possibility of professional insight or wisdom. If we suggest that the only relevant professional expertise is the ability to provide accurate information, we oversimplify the psychology and politics of the professional encounter. If the physician's perceptions, evaluations, and recommendations were all that mattered under the old pater-nalistic system, the new emphasis on patient autonomy threat-ens to make them irrelevant. When this model is pushed to the logical extreme, the physician is not only denied vote but voice.

Why is that so bad? First, professionals are expected to pro-vide support and encouragement as well as information; they are not simply providers of facts. Professionals find themselves responding to requests for advice from persons who are terri-fied and alone; they want to be helpful. In many cases, it is woefully inadequate simply to report the facts and then say, "It's your decision." Thus professional perceptions and value judgments will be relevant, however true it is that they should not settle the issue of forms of care. Most, if not absolutely all, patients care about the judgments and advice of the profes-sionals they work with.

Second, although professionals may not be experts on the value premises held by any particular individual, to function well as professionals they must develop skills at describing and assessing more than simply reporting quantifiable data. Their interpretations of what they see and hear are inevitably evaluative, and they see and hear much more than nonpro-fessionals. At their best they perceive moral as well as biolog-ical portraits of their patients. Of course these portraits are bi-ased to varying degrees, but if we use the possibility of bias as a sufficient reason to rule out someone's testimony, we will have no witnesses left!

Professional power and responsibility are assets, not prob-lems, and professionals may well have important insights. If we want to improve care for the dying, they are a key group to convince, and they are a group from whom others can and are willing to learn. They will be listened to in discussions with patients, in congregations, and in reference to public policy.

What is it about professional perspectives that is most important? For my purposes it is the professionals' perception of the self or soul—their patients' and their own. I am particularly interested in the way they give meaning to their lives, in what is now often called their *spirituality*. I mean to focus on the spirituality of professionals because I think it is inevitably relevant to the kind of care they offer to their patients. If we are clearer about those perceptions and convictions, we will be better placed to understand and improve care for the dying in the United States today.

One of my concerns is with the way professionals perceive—and respect—the spirituality of their dying patients. Thinking that perception is important is scarcely a new idea in professional ethics. Arguably it was the main preoccupation of Paul Ramsey's *The Patient as Person* (1969), even though Ramsey's formulation of it, particularly as it was distilled in his discussion of experimentation with human subjects, tended to reduce the sphere of spirituality to the question of consent. There are not many studies of professionals' perceptions of the spiritual or religious needs and commitments of their patients, however.

Beyond their perceptions of patients I am concerned with the religious and spiritual involvement or commitments of the professionals themselves. Physicians, nurses, social workers, and chaplains have tremendous power to influence care of the dying for good or ill. It is foolish to pretend that their character, spirituality, or religious beliefs are irrelevant to the quality of care that they may provide over time, however important it may be to respect their rights of privacy. As I hope the book will make clear, I do not mean to suggest that we should seek for a new religious orthodoxy among health care providers. Rather, I claim that the state of their souls cannot be entirely separated from their performance in their professional roles.

Moreover, health professionals engaged in care for the dying are doing spiritually demanding work. They are a good test of the vitality of organized religion and the ability of religious communities to provide support to persons who confront some grim aspects of reality daily, occasionally hourly. Saint Paul to the contrary notwithstanding, no religious community can be all things to everyone. But religious communities should not let this particularly important cohort of persons struggle with religious and spiritual issues in isolation, if there is anything they can do to help. The mandate to be vitally concerned with death and care for the dying may be particularly important for Christianity, for at the core of Christian tradition is a crucial death.

My strategy for learning about the spiritual and religious beliefs of health professionals was to enlist the help of a colleague and conduct a series of structured interviews with persons who spend considerable time in care for the dying. A copy of the questions used in those interviews is included as an appendix. We spoke with physicians, nurses, chaplains, and social workers associated with three different hospitals: a level two private nonprofit hospital, a major university medical center complex, and a large Catholic hospital. All but one of our respondents (a rabbi) have been at some time and in some way involved with Christianity, but beneath that loose umbrella their affiliations and spiritualities are remarkably diverse, ranging from zealous evangelical Protestants and traditionally devout Catholics to persons who have little or no inclination ever to darken the door of a church. Our sample is not large—only thirty persons—and each interview lasted only an hour or so. This is not a representative sample of anything, certainly no findings that could claim statistical significance, and I have not produced a detailed ethnographic study of a particular ward, floor, or unit. Any attempt to generalize from these several hundred pages of transcribed conversations faces obvious limits.

However, our interviews do provide a record of a remarkable series of conversations with professionals about questions that matter to them and that should matter to leadership in religion and health care. It amounts to a kind of biopsy of the views and experiences of a diverse, articulate, and accessible group of people.

That exercise in disciplined listening provides the meat of this book, but I have tried to organize the material into an argument—my argument, not one that any of the interviewees made. This is not a strictly ethnographic study; it's more like a report presented to a larger group after an intense series of conversations. But the interview material is important.

Moral conversation should not simply take the form of the professional providing data and the moralist supplying premises and rules of inference. Reflective practice may provide normative insight in at least three forms. First, reflective practitioners may acquire considerable skill at moral description so that their portraits of the issues at stake are more insightful than those any less experienced person could draw. This skill does not necessarily come with experience—professionals can be as obtuse as anyone else—but the possibility of significant insight cannot be ruled out, and one will never get those insightful descriptions unless one takes seriously the responsibility to listen. Moralists should be circumspect about announcing what *the* issues are apart from taking alternative diagnoses into account.

Second, thoughtful professionals are in a unique position to comment on the moral world that they inhabit. First-person accounts are not necessarily the most accurate ones; self-deception is a real possibility, and sometimes others understand us better than we understand ourselves. All that said, if one wants to understand the moral world of any group of people, an obvious first step is listening to what they have to say. We see this point clearly when we think of persons who have frequently been discriminated against such as women or minority group members. Physicians, at least, have not been discriminated against, but listening to their observations is not often seen as a good first move in biomedical ethics. Why should we not acknowledge the importance of listening to them and that their first-person description of what is wrong with care for the dying is a necessary, although certainly not sufficient, component in the moral conversation?

In fact, professional insight may force reexamination of some basic claims of a general frame of reference. To take one very sweeping example: Many of the professionals with whom we spoke have found that they cannot hold to a retributivist theodicy in which the bad things that happen to people are seen as divine punishment for past sins. The conviction they have formed is closely related to their work, their professional observation and experience. In effect their experience makes one set of theological convictions incredible. It is important for religious leaders to know that fact.

Professional rejection of retributivism does not disprove retributivism; indeed, in the minds of those who hold it, it is probably a conviction that cannot be falsified. Nor need one be a physician or nurse to see the problems with that moralistic perspective. My only point is that <u>professional experience can conflict with religious teaching</u>, and it is by no means clear that religious teaching is always the more insightful of the two. Religious ethics and theological ethics can learn from alternative perspectives.

In sum, this book is about moral issues involved in care for the dying; it is a book with two distinctive features. First, it is particularly focused on religion and spirituality; second, I have tried to use the experience of professionals as a source of moral insight. These concerns are more closely related than some may suppose, as spirituality and morality are closely linked in the minds of many persons. Whatever the strict logic of the matter may be, these professionals move smoothly from religious or spiritual concerns to moral convictions. If one attempts to "bleach" the religion out of their morality, very little morality is left. The result is a distorted portrait, vastly underestimating the moral resources that religious persons bring to the moral world. Sticking with actual people makes it hard to forget religion.

In the United States it makes it hard to forget Christianity. In the text that follows I move very easily back and forth between *religion* and *Christianity*. This is not because I hold that Christianity is the only true religion or that it contains the most important insights into care for the dying. My objective is not to "privilege" a particular religious spirituality or the role of religious institutions; rather, I mean to attend to them in their specificity. And I write primarily for a culture in which the remarkably diverse Christian tradition is especially influential. I want to be specific and clear when I think I am appealing to distinctively Christian claims or metaphors; I never want to suggest that *only* Christianity can hold to the claims that I make.

In the next chapter I offer a profile of the respondents, focusing on their religious views, their attitudes toward their own work, and their general views on care for the dying.

The substantive argument begins with chapter 3, in which I find two strategies for coping with unmerited suffering and premature death in the comments of the persons we interviewed. These are fragmentary theodicies. One of them stresses the sovereignty of a transcendent power or God; the other builds on the comfort that comes from the creation of community—

either between God and persons or simply among persons. From this perspective an adequate religious response to suffering entails personal presence with the sufferer, rather than an attempt to explain how suffering fits with God's purposes. Religion should not hope to eliminate all suffering, but it can offer an intellectual and communal context that makes life with suffering more livable.

Chapter 4 tries to spell out the implications of the two fragmentary theodicies for a controverted moral issue—physician-assisted suicide (PAS). Most respondents oppose physician-assisted suicide; I summarize their arguments trying to make some of the connections between religious or spiritual conviction and moral conclusions explicit. They feel a true dilemma: torn between resistance to killing, commitment to relieve suffering, and conviction that the patient's interest is fundamental. Many of the conversation partners favor a situation in which PAS is illegal but covertly practiced in a few cases. I try to make a case for a policy that is more honest and supportive of professionals in hard cases yet faithful to a prohibition on killing.

Both chapters 3 and 4 emphasize the importance of building a robust community within institutions that provide care for dying persons. That concern leads naturally into the argument of chapter 5, which concerns community and conflict. Our respondents tell many stories of conflict: among professionals, among family members, between families and professionals. I try to explain what the religious perspectives of transcendence and community can contribute to the resolution of these conflicts. Religion will not make the conflicts go away; indeed it is often a source of conflict. A community based on superficial agreement can easily be exploitive, however, and I want to argue that a religious perspective that has honestly come to terms with suffering and death is well positioned to serve as a catalyst for community creation. Without good communities in health care settings, hope for improved care for the dying is greatly diminished.

In the last chapter I summarize the argument to that point and then discuss ritual as a key component in community creation and personal support. I think a focus on ritual and community-building is a much more constructive way to argue for the importance of religious sensibilities than attempts to show that prayer and other spiritual practices are clinically helpful; I suggest that religious communities are at their best when they retain a modest vision of their essential contribution to human well-being. I then propose a set of recommendations for action by religious communities to improve both their ministry to dying persons and their contribution to the public discussion of these issues. These recommendations entail educational programs and attention to liturgical and pastoral practice, capitalizing on the experience of professionals within the congregation, judicatory, or denomination. I will also argue that religious communities should take a proactive role in public conversation about care for the dying—proactive in their willingness to help and to learn.

I hope by the end of this short book to have illustrated a distinctively religious perspective on care for the dying and to have suggested ways in which it might be put to use. If the result is to enhance the involvement of American religious communities with care for the dying, that will count as a great success.

Notes

1. American Health Decisions, *The Quest to Die with Dignity: An Analysis of Americans' Values, Opinions and Attitudes Concerning End of Life Care* (Atlanta: American Health Decisions, 1997), 5; see Peter A. Singer, Douglas K. Martin, and Merrijoy

Kelner, "Quality End-of-Life Care: Patients' Perspectives," *JAMA* 281, no. 2 (January 13, 1999); Karen E. Steinhauser, Elizabeth C. Clipp, Maya McNeilly, et al., "In Search of a Good Death: Observations of Patients, Families, and Providers," *Annals of Internal Medicine* 132, no.10 (May 16, 2000): 825–31.

2. Notably the Robert Wood Johnson Foundation's "Faith in Action" program.

3. Robert M. Veatch, "Generalization of Expertise" in *Hasting Center Studies* 1, no. 2 (1973): 29–40.

CHAPTER TWO

~

Conversation Partners

It will be helpful if I introduce the conversation partners before I turn to some issues of particular importance. While they were not promised confidentiality, I want to respect the great candor and openness with which they spoke. So I'm writing at a low level of generality, trying, among other things, to suggest what kinds of persons these people are and what it was like to talk with them about care for the dying.

I was interested in two levels of question. The first concerned the more or less traditional spirituality of the professionals—whether and how they worshipped and what, if any, tradition they had or currently identified themselves with. I call that "traditional" religion, although the spirituality of many persons we talked to is decidedly nontraditional. Secondly, however, I felt it was important to discover their fundamental professional values, for I think that work, as well as religion, is a key shaper of identity. We *identify* ourselves as Reform Jews or Methodists, physicians or nurses. It is certainly logically and psychologically possible for the professional identity and values to dominate the traditional identity and values. I conferred with a group of professionals who have spent a lot of time caring for persons who are dying. What follows is a sketch of what may amount to their professed and de facto deepest commitments. We will see that professional and traditional values play differing roles in the lives of the persons we talked to.

Traditional Religion

All of the professionals interviewed describe themselves as religious or "spiritual." Some are evangelical Christians. Their piety is highly biblical, and the Bible is read to suggest the importance of an adult conversion or act of faith and belief in a life after death with a heavenly reward conditional upon adequate faith and a righteous life today. Another group is religious but more "mainline" in orientation. They worship in Methodist or Presbyterian or Catholic churches; the Bible is somewhat de-centered, and revelation is understood in more sophisticated terms. Traditional religion is clearly part of these people's lives, but it is more explicitly challenged by work experiences, and it does not so clearly function as an authority. It's unclear whether this more integrated notion of traditional and professional values is rooted in personality characteristics of the professionals, or in some core values of the traditions with which they are associated. A third group is best described as "spiritual." While they may occasionally worship in some communal setting, their form of piety is eclectic and idiosyncratic. That is not to say that religion for these persons is trivial or unimportant; this more individual spirituality may be quite intense. Membership in an established community is not central to their identities, however, and their religious engagements have clearly been shaped by a sense of personal need or insight. The self defines spirituality rather than religion defining the self.

Few respondents describe themselves as completely nonreligious; few say that religion as they understand it plays no part in their lives. Not all respondents are positive about existing religious communities or practices. Moreover, almost all of them offer trenchant criticisms of religion in the clinical setting. Nevertheless, it is interesting that few self-consciously define themselves as completely outside the religious circle. (Of course this may say something about Indiana and about the limited sample.)

Our respondents take comfort in their religious beliefs, but to varying degrees and in differing ways. The evangelical professionals live within a structure of belief that clearly sustains them. They have a strong sense of reassurance about their own destiny and that of their patients. In particular they rejoice in belief in a life after death; resurrection in heaven. Death, "the last enemy," has been conquered by Jesus Christ, and that is good news indeed. Religion gives them a system of beliefs that they can use to interpret what is happening to people at the end of life and that helps them to set death into a larger conceptual framework. Religion is closely identified with a particular set of beliefs.

The more mainline Christians, despite their ongoing involvements in a church, find their religious commitment more fluid on the ideological or dogmatic level. Religion for them may not be primarily a matter of beliefs and ideas. It may relate more closely to a set of attitudes toward other persons and the world; to a point it relates to membership in an ongoing community of worshipers. Thus when we asked whether religion "provides them with help" in coping with death and dying, the crisp answer that the evangelicals can give is not available to the "mainliners." Religion may not offer ideological or dogmatic support; rather, it might help them by sustaining another dimension of life, one that serves both to change the subject and provide a broader and richer perspective through which tragedies at the end of life can be re-visioned. As we will see, whatever the roots of their loyalties, these professionals have remained with the "mainline" communities by choice. They neither work out a full independent spirituality nor accept a very traditional view.

The spiritual professionals we interviewed have worked out a form of loyalty or way of finding meaning in life that is tailored to their own needs. Thus it would be very strange if it did not provide our respondents with some help, or if it were seriously challenged by events at the bedside. For some, the spiritual may involve walking or hiking; it may involve intense recreation; it may include other people who see the world in somewhat the same way.

The religious or spiritual views of a great majority of these professionals have changed over time. Several patterns stand out.

One is searching for a better community of the same kind when the old one seems to go sour. "My whole family goes to the same church. We have a relatively new minister, and I just can't seem to relate. Big difference between the pastor I grew up with and the new one. The one I grew up with was the kind of warm, huggy person that you always felt like you could talk to. This guy is more intellectual. Very bright, funny, but I don't feel like there's a connection. And that's been a piece that I needed that I just haven't had. So we're kind of church shopping. They started a new service at our church; the music is different. You don't have to get dressed up to go to church and that kind of thing. Mostly our goal at this point, having two children, you know, [is] wanting them to at least be exposed so they can make their own choices. I so much enjoyed being raised in the church. I said my prayers every single night to myself. I said the same ones. When the kids were little, I said the prayers with them. And unfortunately, recently that seems to have kind of gone away a little bit. The [really difficult] thing is just trying to come to grips with 'Is it okay for me to want to get something out of church?' As opposed to [going because I should]. It's always been really hard for me to ask for something. I had this feeling that I wasn't really supposed to ask for anything."

Something of the same uncertainty and looking for a better community characterize this physician, who was asked if he was raised in a religiously observant home. "We went to church almost every Sunday. My father was a Southern Baptist, and my mother was a Methodist, so we mostly went to the Methodist church. And pretty regularly. I didn't go to church in college, except when I took a singing job in one of the choirs in town, so I went every Sunday and sang. [But] I don't sing much any more. I've kind of had a falling out with my church that I go to here, and we haven't been in a long time. But it's nothing about the religion. It just was the church and the preacher, primarily. But I consider myself a Christian and an overall good person, I guess."

This seeking may go along with pretty active involvement in a community, as it appeared when I asked one Catholic nurse if she considered herself to be "observant." "Oh, yeah. I'm a cantor at my church. And my two sisters are nuns. So I come from a real strong Irish Catholic family. But I think I've broken out of the total Catholic [scene]. I'm much more interested in what other belief systems are about. I don't know that I understand very well, but I try to be much more tolerant of those things, broaden it out to a belief in a higher power, if you will. But my own personal traditional belief is the traditional Catholic background."

All these professionals are persons I think of as of the "main line," but they all are looking for something beyond what a given congregation or denomination may have to offer. Yet none of them has gone so far as to make a radical change in tradition or to sever all ties with organized religious communities. Some of the persons we interviewed, however, started in one tradition, left it, then found a different spiritual home. One social worker, for example, said she "started off very religious [Presbyterian]. But about sixth grade we moved, and there was a big gap in my life. And actually just this past year is when I started getting back involved in the church again. And it was a big, big gap for me. [Religion is] a way to process and deal with death. And to be honest, that's one of the main reasons that brought me back to religion, just having some type of framework to be able to put everything in. And it helps me draw boundaries and make my own personal boundaries so I don't get burned out doing what I do. I wouldn't call myself real religious. I'm actually converting, becoming Catholic. And I'm going through classes for that. My husband is Catholic, and I wasn't when we were married. And my main need is trying to find a structure and just thinking of what happens to people after they've died. And also how families find strength to get through that."

Yet another trajectory is moving through traditions to come out with something quite personal: "I differentiate between religious belief and faith. So the exercise of religion within a specific, doctrinal kind of thing is not as important to me as keeping my faith life and my spirituality as vibrant as possible and keeping as connected as possible with the spiritual power that is available to me, the grace that's there, the spiritual energy that I can describe as God. Some people are uncomfortable with that, but for me God's okay. God is either nongendered or a woman, if I have to be answerable or think about it. And that's real different from the tradition I grew up in." Another social worker, after noting that she was raised a Southern Baptist, said, "I think my religious belief has changed. As I was growing up, it seemed to me there was a tremendous amount of hypocrisy in the so-called Christian world and the only divergent groups in my little town where I grew up in North Carolina were Baptists and Presbyterians. And they couldn't even get together for a joint Thanksgiving service."

She continued, "I lived with my sister for two years, and her husband was an Episcopal minister. So I was exposed to that particular brand of religion, but I was not that involved with it. And then when I married, I married a Jewish person. And I took instruction in Judaism and was actually given a Jewish name and so on. But then, he wasn't interested in practicing. So when we had children, we started going to the Unitarian Church. And that was probably to save them from the Presbyterian neighbor across the street. And after the children lost interest, we still kept active in the Unitarian Church. But I suppose if I had to characterize myself now, it would be a lapsed Unitarian. So I don't know if you can be any more lapsed than that. I think of myself as a person with spiritual values [such as continuity of life] but not a strong identification with one church or another. The works that we do are measured more here on earth, on what we do with the people that we interact with, rather than future rewards."

Particularly among the physicians, this working out of a personal spirituality may lead to something approaching skepticism. One physician, when asked if he was raised in a religious tradition, said, "I was raised in the Episcopal Church. I don't know if you know the Episcopal Church, but it's not a lot of hand holding, especially in the '50s and '60s. It was a very sterile environment. You know, they played classical music and that was it. And I don't go to church now. I consider myself a very spiritual person but not a quote 'religious' person. And I really haven't gotten a lot of my feeling from church teachings. I don't know where my values came from. I don't know how much of it I got from the church or any of that. But I would describe myself as more of a humanist rather than I believe in magic among people. I believe in spiritual things. I believe there are things greater. And I've gotten a lot of it from my patients. Their own beliefs, how strong they felt about things. So I'm not an atheist. I think I believe in spirituality."

He was asked if his patients talk to him about their or his religious beliefs. "I think they do, especially with death and dying. We don't here in the office. Very few people come and talk about their feelings in my office, unless we're talking about death or dying or some terrible thing that has happened or is going to happen. And then I think people do talk to me, and they want to know if I believe in God. Most of them ask me if I do, if they're religious." What do you answer them? "I tell them that I do, because I don't think they would understand if I said I was a spiritual person. So I tell them that I do, but I don't practice it. I tell them that I do believe in God. I do believe in a higher vision, a greater being, things that are above man." This thoughtful physician feels he must keep his own personal beliefs in the closet.

Religious or spiritual values may be seen as strictly instrumental, albeit not unimportant. For example, another physician when asked about his religious life said, "I struggle in my own mind with science as a religion, as a way of knowing truth versus beliefs based on faith, unprovable tenets. And I've always wrestled with that. I continue to this day to wrestle with that. I don't want to insult anybody in a religious belief, but I think so much of it is myth. And I mean myth in the true sense of man's storytelling to explain existence. The value to me of religion is instillation of value systems. There's a lot I don't like about religious denominations, but at the same time, I recognize that life without values is the classic boat without a rudder. And how we get those values instilled in us, I think, is very important. My wife and I have that same issue as you raise a child. We have a ten-year-old. What values do we want him to have? You just can't go through life going 'There is no right or wrong.' If you did that, you would have no course. Your steering linkage is broken. I think rather than make it harder or easier on those beliefs, my practice challenges me to constantly think about those things. I enjoy that. I don't like to go and put in a day's work and be just like an assembly line worker. We're dealing with real important issues. You know, life/death are obvious, but people's loss of function, loss of livelihood, pain, things that just affect you to the very core of your existence. Mental illness. You know, on and on and on. And I think that you have to have a value system, or you don't make it through a day without it."

For some the start was eclectic or nontraditional but a provisional home has been found in a tradition. "My dad's Hindu. Never practiced. And my mother is Mormon. And we periodically went to church with my mother, but it was only when my father was in a good enough mood to let go. Because he didn't believe in the whole thing. And so it was sort of an on-and-off kind of thing. I don't think I ever had deep convictions about religion until I left home and went to graduate school. And at that point, I think, is when I decided what was right and not right and chose not to be Hindu or Mormon." Was your father mistaken, because you've found religion does play a role in your life today? "Oh, yeah. Pretty much guides what I do." So, "Do you think of yourself as a religious person?" "Oh, I don't know. I hate that word, 'religious person.' Tell me what you think your religious person is. Am I a Bible reader? No. But you know, do I read my Bible? Yes. Do I pray every day? Yes. Do I go to church? Yes. Am I teaching my kid the values that I believe in? Yes." So what church is it? "Baptist."

This nurse doesn't think she conforms to her image of what a religious person is, despite the fact that she engages in more traditional practices than most members of traditional congregations. We asked her which, if any, of her religious beliefs were most relevant to her work in care for the dying. "I think probably just the whole thing of respect for everything and everybody. And that God created everything. And by virtue of that, everything deserves respect and is sacred, including dying patients. And I think that probably has guided me more than anything. I mean, there are days that you just don't want to go in and clean up that poop one more time. But you know what? That is God's child, and he loves that person. And so that probably more than anything."

A nurse who was asked if she was raised in a religious home displays a similar trajectory. "Actually not. It's funny how I got involved with religion. My parents were not 'religious.' They didn't go to church or anything, although my mom certainly believed in the hereafter. And I got involved in the church because as a kid, I was raised in what I call the boondocks, and there was nothing to do. So we started going to church because that was something to do. And you know, even as a young child, I remember feeling that there was more to this than just going to church. And of course I really didn't make a commitment until I was an older adult. I was in my twenties. But I remember thinking that there's more to this, but I was afraid to do it because I thought you had to be perfect, you know, to make a commitment. And I learned in my older years, really, no one is perfect, you know." A religious community has provided this woman with a spiritual home she would not otherwise have had.

Still others have grown within a particular tradition. One Catholic physician said: "In my attempts to find a way to be balanced, I found out that what's more important is to be centered. I'm trying now to center myself, or ground myself, if you will. It involves a lot of prayer and meditation. I used to try to meditate, and it helped me when I was in college. Just a kind of an Eastern form of meditation. But [I] couldn't stick with it, and whenever I returned to it, I couldn't stick with it. So I went to a medical meeting where they had a workshop on meditation. They had a seminar where a Trappist monk named Thomas Keating was the speaker. He calls his activity 'centering prayer,' as opposed to meditation, but they are very similar. The twenty to thirty minutes twice a day of meditation where you sit quietly. This practice has opened up a lot for me, and so it made my kind of traditional upbringing much more meaningful. Before this happened, I may or may not go to church on a Sunday. And since this it's rare for me to miss Mass each day and I try to find the time to meditate every morning, and then it's harder in the evening, but I try to find the time."

For most of these professionals religion and spirituality are arenas for growth and change. They can identify what they once believed and how they worshiped; often that is different from their current practice. Religion or spirituality have not been constants for them; they have changed. Going along with this, religious institutions are seldom looked to for either comfort or teaching by the evangelicals or the mainline professionals. In fact, the closest thing to an exception to this rule in our sample is a "spiritual" nurse who found great help in a somewhat unconventional church. We discovered at least one Christian support or prayer group among the evangelicals in the work setting, but that is clearly separated from regular congregational worship. To be sure, the fact that our respondents didn't say that they find comfort in regular worship or other congregational activities doesn't prove that they don't. They may not have thought about it, and our questions may not have elicited this information. But if this connection were vital, one would expect some evidence to appear in the interviews.

Respondents were not only unlikely to have a secure and permanent home in a congregation; they were unlikely to turn to clergy when they need someone to talk to. They may have concluded that the clergy are rigid, inexperienced, or insecure, or they may not believe that a member of the clergy might have something to bring to the conversation. Chaplains get better marks, largely because they show up and because they have learned to listen and to avoid superficial platitudes. However, chaplains who come in with too strong an agenda of their own, unwilling to listen and spend time, are quickly written off not only by physicians and nurses but also by the other chaplains. Chaplains feel that they must have come to terms with their own mortality, and then be willing to listen. As one told us, "I make a fairly good living not knowing what to say next."

Professional Spirituality

Professional identity may serve as a religious surrogate (or as a religion) for many professionals. Our attempts to follow up this lead produced mixed results. We found work identity to be powerful but less all-encompassing than we had supposed. We had imagined that many health professionals, physicians in particular, would take what we might call an idolatrous stance toward their work and that they would be driven, obsessive people. In particular we supposed that this identity would determine their attitudes toward care of the dying, but if that is so the vitalist commitment to preserve life at all cost was far in the background for our respondents. Instead other more specific professional values were in higher profile.

Physicians

The notion of medicine as a calling is significant in the lives of many physicians and determinative for some. One doctor we spoke with remembered having been told in college "if you are not going to be a priest, the next best thing is a doctor." And it is a line of work that entails self-respect. One doctor said, "It's a profession that deals with tough issues and doesn't turn chicken." However, it is clear that for many physicians medicine is just a job. A surprising number in our sample see a need to "get a life" outside the professional realm, and all of our respondents have distinctive sets of interests and strong family commitments. They may worship at the shrine of the gods of medicine, but they pay homage elsewhere as well.

More striking than unqualified focus on their work was the physicians' individualism. They are self-directed. They may choose to go to church; they may find spiritual support in some nontraditional activity. But they will make up their own minds about it, and they are not particularly influenced by general social expectations. This is understandable. Doctors must learn to rely on individual perception and judgment in diagnosis and prescription. Judgment calls are made many times a day, if not an hour. Physicians develop the habit of making up their own minds on the basis of their own experience and observation and then of having others take their judgments seriously.

Moreover, it is a cliché of the literature of the sociology of medicine that physicians are trained for "detached concern," that is, to look at things objectively and to avoid wishful thinking. Some will talk about the "art" of medicine, but that is never a substitute for coming to conclusions supported by good studies and the evidence. Thus, consultation with other physicians occurs, but it tends to be consultation on the hard data of diagnosis and prescription. Less objective matters—for example, best ways to treat or talk to the dying—seem to the physicians to be largely matters of opinion, where any one person's viewpoint is as good as another's.

When we asked, "Who do you talk to about the bad times, about the deaths, about the disappointments?" we got a range of answers. Chaplains talk to spouses, colleagues, nurses; they seek help in many places. Nurses talk to each other; peer groups are terribly important. But physicians tend to talk only with their spouses, if anyone. They don't talk to chaplains, they don't talk to nurses, and they don't talk to each other. There are important exceptions to this; one physician, who works in an innovative and interdisciplinary setting, gets a lot of help from "our team meetings . . . and a lot of dark humor" and that sentiment was echoed by two other physicians who are in different, but comparably interdisciplinary and focused, forms of practice. Still, our interviews suggest that medicine is a lonely profession.

A second important point about the spirituality of the physicians we interviewed is that they all expect not only to cure but also to be able to provide effective symptom control. They are hard on other doctors who fail to offer that comfort, and they are also critical of what they perceive to be overtreatment, whether it is forced on a physician by family, by their (mis)perception of the requirements of the law, or by some other factor. They are bitterly critical of habits that discourage adequate pain medication. Knowing when to stop and knowing how to help with troubling symptoms are highly valued skills.

For example, one geriatrician we spoke with said, "The comfort part of the business is [too often] swept over by the disease-curing part of the business. You see, in geriatrics, we've come to understand we don't *cure*[1] anyone, other than for the occasional bladder infection or whatever. Our patients all have burdens of chronic illness from which they don't recover. You can manage them, you can help them, you can improve them, you can balance them out, but you can't cure them. Most doctors still are [completely] in the curing business. People that need care at the end of life represent a failure of their ability to cure them. And so they kind of get prioritized down the list. I don't think overtly. You can spend your time trying to cure a bunch of people, or you can work with these people over here that you can't cure. And so a bunch of people spend their time with those that they think they can still cure." He gets at this point by saying "medicine [meaning attempts to cure] is not good for old people, but they need it [i.e., other forms of medically informed assistance] anyway."

Our sample thinks that palliative care skills are not as widespread as their fellow physicians think they are. Moreover, personal or relational skills are crucial. We asked what they thought was the worst mistake a physician could make in care for the dying. One said it was saying there is no hope, or "almost as bad," saying, "There is nothing more I can do for you." "I think it's perfectly responsible to say 'I can't cure your disease and I am limited in what I can do.' The patient wants to hear that you'll do what you can, that you will keep them comfortable, that you will keep them as informed as possible, and that you will allow them to have some control over what happens to them."

Another said he thought the most common mistake by physicians who care for the dying was "being physician-centered instead of patient-centered. We make patients play our game by our rules, as opposed to making our approach patient-centered or family-centered." But the worst mistake is "lack of compassion, being hurried, being unwilling or unable to listen. Doctors often have a difficult time communicating with patients. They have a difficult time listening. Studies show that the average amount of time a patient is given to respond to a question from the doctor is like twelve seconds before they are interrupted." The effect, he thinks, is to avoid any real engagement between physician and patient. These communication failures may unintentionally engender a feeling of "abandonment" on the part of patients. Understandably physicians often simply don't know what to say. But the effect of communication failures is to leave families in the dark, wrestling with their own lack of understanding of what is going on and what they might expect. These physicians believe that this is uncaring and unprofessional.

Nurses[2]
We found nurses' identities to be more complex and social than those of physicians. Interpersonal and social skills are stressed much more strongly. As Daniel Chambliss and others have noted, nurses serve many masters: patients, hospitals, physicians. Many people who train as nurses do not continue to practice nursing throughout their working lives. This phenomenon may well suggest disappointment or frustrations with the profession. Today, because of health care financing and scheduling trends, many nurses are unable to provide the kind of personal care that they would like to.

Nurses believe that our expectations of medicine and nursing are quite different. No one will fault a nurse for the fact that someone dies under her care—so long as the technical assignment has been handled properly—but they will certainly fault a physician for an unanticipated death. "[F]or physicians . . . it's harder to let go. Because they are supposed to be saving people, not letting them die." "Nurses are always concerned about symptom management . . . comfort . . . Physicians are trained to look at the medical management of the condition."

Nurses' perception of what care for the dying entails is profoundly realistic. The well-known SUPPORT study reports that one nurse commented, "[W]e were not there to change the course . . . length . . . or depth of the river or the turbulence of the river—all we could do was to try to keep the leaves floating down the stream from getting so tangled with one another that they couldn't appreciate the journey."[3]

Therefore, the nurses we spoke with regarded the nurse's ability to provide personal presence as the single most important contribution they can make to the care of the dying. They define the patient's biggest expectation as "our attention," and they find that expectation entirely reasonable. "[T]he most they expect is a sense of presence. Just a moment to be engaged with the patient and family. . . . [S]ome families . . . [want] a lot of information and data . . . [but] once you have given them that and they realize that there is no other place to go except be here, then it is a matter of presence and just being with them."

Personal presence entails the creation of something like family bonds. "I have become friends with a lot of patients that I take care of often. . . . [W]e tend to latch on to those that are our age, that we can relate to. . . . We get to know their . . . children by first name, and their parents and brothers and sisters, and it's kind of a family." Seriously ill patients become comfortable with a given nurse, and "we want these patients to be ours, not a float nurse who probably doesn't understand or really, truly love . . . the field that we are in." It is not clear that all the nurses in our sample have or want to have this level of relationship; it is clear that they all think that personal caring and the presence that it connotes are central to quality nursing care for the dying.

The nurses are frustrated that they cannot always meet that expectation. Probably the most experienced nurse in our sample regrets that nurses no longer do enough of the "good old basic emotional, physical care . . . [for example] if you're in pain, instead of running and getting you a shot, maybe giving you a back rub, sitting down, holding your hand. And it's not that nurses don't want to do that. We just don't have the time anymore." Another thinks patients don't understand the strains that nurses are under; it's unreasonable in the present context "if they want us to be in the room a lot. And I find myself apologizing to them that I can't be there more for them." Another nurse commented, "[O]ne of the biggest frustrations for all of us is that we don't have time to take care of our patients. To sit down and talk to them. I mean more about what's going on with them emotionally and then spiritually. Because you are passing pills and doing treatments, and you've got people throwing up and people who are in pain."

Their frustrations relate not only to the realistic hopes they may have for their patients but also to other systemic problems. Patients are moved from unit to unit, breaking continuity of care; they may be assigned to an inappropriate unit. Even if they stay on the same floor, many nurses now work twelve-hour shifts, working only three days a week. "[E]specially with nurses working twelve-hour shifts, I don't think you have that bond with *a* nurse anymore, if you're a patient. Because you have different nurses all the time." Some issues are peculiar to tertiary care settings, where patients may have unrealistically high expectations of miracle cures. In general, nurses increasingly find themselves serving as managers. Thus, when we asked our respondents if they would advise one of their own children to go to nursing school, one answered flatly, "No. I think it's too hard to be a good nurse in this health care world . . . [because] a lot of what nursing is right now is managing people and things. And if they are going to manage people and things, they might as well work Monday through Friday, eight to five, in an office and make a lot of money doing it."

Chaplains

These clergy have a dual loyalty: to tradition and religious community, on the one hand, and to the hospital and health care on the other. Their relationship to tradition and religious communities is fraught with ambivalence. All the chaplains we spoke to are in this form of ministry by choice; they see chaplaincy as a specialized kind of ministry that requires certain kinds of gifts. One analogized it to the difference between a surgeon and a general practitioner. Congregational ministry, he said, is like being a GP; becoming a chaplain amounts to a decision to specialize. Nostalgia for a parish or congregation is not found among these men (and our sample was all males). They tend to think that congregational ministers are overwhelmed with trivialities, "stoned to death with popcorn," as one of them put it. They are proud that they are dealing with people at times of desperation and times that matter.

On the question of their own personal religious or spiritual life and involvement with a traditional congregation, they are almost as diverse as the general population. All are nominally members of a congregation, but exactly what that means varies greatly among them. At least one is regularly and energetically involved. Most are not. Most of them are very self-conscious about possible turf issues in their professional relationship with congregational clergy; they are aware that they know only a snapshot of the lives of most of the patients to whom they minister.

They want to be involved with people in trouble. Ministry in other contexts includes celebrations such as weddings, baptisms, or bar mitzvahs. But the hospital is not a place of joy; it is a place of sadness. "The hospital is a culture of sickness. . . . It's not typically a positive place. I mean, there are recoveries but typically we don't get in on the celebratory end of the recoveries." One of the chaplains estimates that 50 percent of his work is dealing with death; another recalls working nights when he helped with decisions and bereavement for seven or eight deaths per night; still a third dealt with 158 deaths in his first year.

Although they like their work, these chaplains are almost as ambivalent about the hospital as the church. On the one hand, it gives them a setting in which they can do something that matters. On the other hand, it is foreign space, and not their space. "You're not working in your own ballpark. That's the church . . . you're working in the physicians' and in the nurses' kind of place." Still, they tend to identify with it more than with the world of the local congregation. In the New Testament phrase, they are certainly in the hospital world; whether they are of that world is a harder question, and they sometimes seem to go native.

They see themselves as having ministries to professionals as well as to patients. One notes that physicians come around the patient less after a terminal diagnosis and surmises that this is from a sense of futility rather than from fear of death. They have compassion for physicians but see them as the source of many of the spiritual and moral problems of nurses and pa-tients; their own relations with nurses are easier than with physicians. One of them captures part of what they all feel when he says that his role as chaplain is "support to the on-line ministry . . . the nurses are the on-line ministry." Nurses, he thinks, have a less bounded role than physicians; they are more involved with a range of general issues that are intimate. Chaplains, in contrast, are distinctively associated with death. Patients "don't mind acting out behavior that's socially inap-propriate around nurses but are far more reticent . . . around the chaplain."

One chaplain clearly defined his role as support for nurses who were, he thought, the primary ministers in health care.

He had not stopped ministering to patients, but he acknowledged the limited amount and quality of patient contact he could have. To him, good stewardship meant investing his time in a way that would have the most significant impact on patients, and that meant providing pastoral support for nurses. Nurses don't always and only get rave reviews from chaplains, however. Many are "passive aggressive," according to one chaplain, who continues, "they are with patients more than physicians, and therefore 'have to clean up,'" but "they are very driven also, and they may not hear the patient. They can get involved in the technical business of doing the nursing and discount the patient too."

Only one of the chaplains we interviewed is clearly proactive about raising explicitly religious issues. One reason he likes his current position is that it allows him freedom to do that. The physicians at the hospital where he works are open to discussion of the spiritual side of things; some are clearly comfortable praying with their patients. "I consider myself a kind of spiritual care specialist. But by no means am I the only professional who can provide spiritual care. In fact, I think part of my role is to empower other professionals to do that." Consistent with this role, he will occasionally ask a patient, "Are you all right with God?"—something that it seems unlikely any other of these chaplains would do. Nevertheless he rejects evangelism and thinks the worst mistake a chaplain can make is "preaching a patient to heaven . . . a kind of salvific agenda with the patient."

The dominant mode among these chaplains is appreciation for spiritual and religious diversity. Chaplaincy is no place, one of the chaplains told us, for a denominational ministry. A Protestant, he claimed to know of an instance of a rabbi offering communion. Their ministries are neither tightly confessional nor heavily invested with traditional concepts. They don't preach. Their crucial role is "being present," which entails listening. Sometimes it just means being in the room with someone who is also silent. It is true that they want hospitals to honor value commitments that, in the case of two hospitals where these chaplains are based, are explicitly religious. But for them that affirmation of particularity is the ground for celebration of diversity.

Asked to identify the worst mistake a chaplain can make, they say giving "pat answers," allowing death to "become routine." One stressed the importance of being reflective, saying the worst mistake would be "not to do my own work about what this means to me and so then to be superficial with a patient or family." Another said it would be "to presume to know the patient's suffering or the family dynamics." Dodging the real work that needs to be done can occur by "giving medical advice." Their notion of ministry is highly personalistic, stressing a search for authenticity in presence and a real commitment to be with patients whenever they are wanted. Accordingly, they have much clearer convictions on relationship issues than on the issues of moral decision making. For example, although their positions on physician-assisted suicide are diverse, none of them gives a crisp conceptual account of why he thinks what he does. Yet they are very articulate, sensitive, and thoughtful about how the dying should be cared for and about issues associated with conversations with patients, families, and professionals. Compared to academics and many physicians, they have little patience with the splitting of hairs, but they see the big picture unusually well.

This breadth of vision means that the chaplains are very sensitive to socioeconomic issues. They are concerned about access and income differentials. And they are aware of the economic status of their own profession. "Advising someone to go into ministry in a capitalistic culture is to acknowledge the fact that you're going to be a highly trained professional who is not going to be in the mainstream of economic reality."

In summary, our sample shows considerable diversity within a narrow set of external parameters. All are practicing in Indiana; for all but one the religious tradition with which they have been involved is Christianity. But their stories reveal striking changes over time. They have moved from one religious community to another one or from lack of religious involvement to intense commitment. Some have left a tradition to move into more self-defined forms of spirituality or continued a particular external commitment but deepened their personal involvement.

The professional groups differ from each other and there are differences within each of the groups. Still one can offer some generalizations about each group. Physicians tend to be individualists, data and result driven. The physicians we interviewed, by design an atypical sample, are critical of their professional colleagues who cannot—or at any rate often do not—provide effective palliative and humane care at the end of life. Nurses see themselves as likely to have a broader vision, but they struggle with inadequate time, and worry that they have in fact become managers and crisis helpers rather than providers of ongoing and informed personal care. Chaplains live on the border between the world of religion or spirituality and the world of the hospital. They make their living listening and trying to be present to patients and professionals. They can be very critical of physicians, nurses, and local churches.

I turn now to identifying some particularly important issues in conversations with these professionals.

Notes

1. Emphasis added.

2. "Professional Commitment to Personal Care: Nurses' Commitments to Care for the Dying," in *Caring Well: Religion, Narrative, and Health Care Ethics*, ed. David H. Smith (Louisville, Ky.: Westminster John Knox Press, 2000).

3. Elizabeth F. Hiltunen, Cynthia Medich, Susan Chase, et al., "Family Decision Making for End of Life Treatment: The Support Nurse Narratives," *The Journal of Clinical Ethics* (1998): 1–13.

CHAPTER THREE

~

Explaining and Justifying

What makes a life good or meaningful? On what, if anything, are human beings dependent? What, if any, powers should we hold in awe or reverence? Never are these issues more acute than at times when death is in prospect, for death calls our very identities into question. I want to begin by examining our interviewees' comments about the question of the meaning of life in the face of suffering. When many of them think of religion they think of a monotheistic God. Belief in such a god may be an asset or a liability when death approaches. For example, is God a person? It is hard to have the comfort of thinking of God as someone who personally cares for us without having the liability of thinking of our misfortunes as having been chosen by God.

Death may not come on time, and when the person who dies is young, or important to us, or virtuous or full of promise—or for any one of many other reasons—the untimeliness of death can be particularly hard. How could a good God allow this to happen—to her, to him, or to me? So far as we can see, God is either not as good as we'd like or not as powerful as we'd like. These facts force religious persons to question God's justice, or love, or power. Many of the "spiritual" professionals with whom we spoke do not think in traditional theistic terms, but they too have to confront the problem of lives that are cut short or end miserably. We talked to people who daily, sometimes hourly, confront situations in which the good die young, and it makes no sense to attempt to fit events into a coherent picture of a rational universe. Yet these people continue to think of themselves as religious. I will briefly summarize a few of their comments and try to develop or respond to major themes in my own voice.

Anger and Incomprehension

The first responses our respondents had to untimely and bad deaths included frustration, disappointment, and an inability neatly to fit what they'd heard into a vision of the world they found sensible. Sometimes there are explanations; justifications are harder to come by. One physician said, "I don't understand why a lot of bad things happen. I never will. Those are what I call questions for God, and I store them up. So one of these days I can talk to whoever and say 'Why this, why this, why this?'" Another doctor said, "My feeling about the role of God in this world, I think, is probably different from many people's. I have a great deal of difficulty in understanding how people can say things like, 'Well, this tragic accident was God's will. It's part of God's plan.' Perhaps it is. Perhaps I don't understand. I prefer to think that God has put all this in motion and given us resources and tools and intellect and things to work with. And then we do the best we can."

One nurse said, "It always seems to be the nicer, sweeter families that have death. And you see these not-so-nice characters that just seem to go on forever. And so sometimes you wonder like, 'Why do the good ones go?' Or 'Why does someone young have to go through this?'" Another, when asked if her work challenged her religious beliefs, said, "It does sometimes. When we have a mom with six-, seven-, eight-year-olds at home and she's only thirty-three with breast cancer that has metastasized, you do wonder, Exactly what is God doing? And why is He doing that to this person? Why is He leaving those three children without a mother? When we have group and when I have to sit back and think about it alone, it's God's plan, you know. And I try not to question what he's doing. You know, there has to be a purpose."

Predictably, perhaps, the chaplains have the most to say on this issue. From the rabbi: "Certainly there are a lot of things in traditional theology and belief that would be challenged by the kind of things that I see every day. People have all these clichés: that God never sends you anything that you are not strong enough to handle. And God is perfect in terms of always doing the right thing and stuff like that. Look around, and you see that there are bad things happening out there. And if God is in control, why do these happen? And if God is good, why do these things happen? So you certainly question that. But again, coming from the Jewish tradition, I come from the experience of the Holocaust. Millions of people were killed for no reason except for hate and intolerance. And many of them were very pious people. How do you believe in a good God after that experience?"

A Christian chaplain talked about the death of a child on Christmas morning. "I remember feeling anger toward God despite my intellectual reasoning. You know, God's not up there pulling strings. It was such an affront and felt so unfair and so cruel if God did have any control over people dying and people living. . . . It was very difficult, very challenging to me religiously. But then you think about the Holocaust and all these other things on a much larger scale that we as a society have had to try to reason through and in a sense, what happened that Christmas morning kind of pales in comparison."

Another Christian chaplain says, "I think it's critical to the grief process that persons express anger with God. And I think the 'My God, my God, why hast Thou forsaken me?' phrase of Christ is an expression of anger and abandonment and betrayal and therefore gives any person of faith the carte blanche to react the same way. You know, with their feelings of abandonment and aloneness and isolation and fear and anger."

I asked one chaplain if patients ask theological or religious questions. He said, "Sometimes, although it's no requirement, you know." "What sort of things along that line might they ask?" "I remember a guy when I first entered CPE who was an early Hodgkin's disease patient. And after I got to know him a little bit, he said, 'Now,' he said, 'do you think that God gave me this disease?' And I said, 'No, I really don't.' He said, 'You know, my oncologist says if God does this to people, he must be a real son of a bitch.' And I said, 'Well, I guess there is a good reason to be angry.' I said, 'Do you believe that?' He said, 'No, I don't believe that.' I said, 'Well, what do you believe?' 'Well,' he said, 'I don't know what to believe about it. I kind of think God will take care of me whatever happens.' And of course, he died. I kind of believe like he did. I think he taught me a lot."

God as More than Judge or Teacher

It is a sign of the resilience or stubbornness of religion that these thoughtful people remain religious while articulating these views. One logical way to handle these problems is to discard the concept of God. But that's something that most of the people we talked to can't, or won't, do. "Maybe I don't deny God because I have to have somebody to be angry at. I don't know. There have been times when I have wondered: What if there isn't a God? I don't know how to explain it, so in some ways I guess I still hold on to some of the old God answers. God's the answer to the questions I can't find answers to, which is a pretty poor theology, I think. And the other side of that is that even in my times of doubt and anger, I can't not believe in God. In fact, one of the things that sometimes has made me angry is I've felt like God has had such a hold on me that God won't let go of me. And I would like for God to let go of me. Just leave me alone. And I cannot escape the sense that God is here and is a part of me, and I'm a part of God. And I think that's true of all people."

These comments also make clear that some frequent religious responses to suffering will strike these persons as wrong, even perverse. For example, to suggest that suffering is a justified punishment for someone's past mistakes, or that we have to suffer in order to grow, will seem to be inadequate. It is true that illness may be self-caused and that persons pay health-related prices for the moral shortcomings of their parents or society. People do have responsibilities for the state of their own and others' health. But the causal nexus is complicated, and only rarely is there one cause to which all the evil can be traced, a cause inexplicable in terms of prior events over which an agent had no control. We've all known persons who have died of the consequences of smoking. Should he have quit? Of course. Is the fact that he was unable to quit simply his fault? Rarely. And that is an easy case.

Similarly, people do learn through disappointment and suffering. We might even agree that someone who hasn't suffered at all (if there be such persons) lives an impoverished life from which the richness of human fulfillment is omitted.

But suffering can crush as well as ennoble the spirit. People are not always able to rise to the occasion.

The point is not to discourage people from taking responsibility for their own health and for that of others, or to imply that all suffering is to be avoided. To the contrary, there are sufferings we should endure, and we should be willing to accept responsibility when we cause others to suffer. But these facts should not lead us to think that God is trying to punish us or teach us a lesson by making bad things happen. And I believe that the reason the persons we interviewed so clearly reject the moral or pedagogical explanations of suffering is the extraordinary disproportion that they see between the suffering of a few and any possible harm they might have done or lesson that they or others might learn. I think we might try to develop their insights in something like the following ways.

In general, tragedy seems to be the least inadequate category to describe the spiritual crisis that suffering entails. Speaking of *tragedy*, Margaret Mohrmann notes, forces us to think of specific persons who suffer and die and of their histories; it raises questions about choices made and self-examination; it makes clear that we are unable fully to explain or justify what happens. It "seems to endow the events with a transcendent seriousness, while at the same time allowing, even requiring, them to exceed the limits of comprehensibility."[1]

Can the inexplicability itself be explained? When we use the scriptural metaphor of human beings as "children of God," we may think of God as our parent who rightly scolds or teaches us. But this makes the difference between ourselves and God too small. As Marilyn McCord Adams remarks, we often imagine the relationship on the model of teenagers (humans) and their parents (God). But the better analogy, Adams suggests, is between God as parent and us as *infant* children. There is a great "size gap" between God and persons. We and

God are not "moral peers" for whom the problem may be solved as we, the children, grow older. The reality is that our partial explanations of the terrible things that happen will never be more than partial. In effect, the moralistic categories of God as moral judge or moral educator presume that we know more about God than we can ever claim to know.[2]

Adams goes on to observe that preoccupation with moral categories for understanding the relationship between persons and God leads us into attempts to explain or justify "horrendous evils" in moral terms. But that is impossible. She finds insight in use of categories of "purity and defilement" and "honor and shame," but her core proposal is that our salvation from horrendous evils comes from our relationship to the good God. "For what is good for a person is for him/her to be appropriately related to great enough goods. . . . If Divine Goodness is infinite, if intimate relation to It is thus incommensurably good for created persons, then we have identified a good big enough to defeat horrors in every case."[3] Adams is not talking about an abstract relationship. She insists that persons must be aware of God's goodness to them if their sufferings are to be redeemed, so she must postulate immortality.

The striking thing about Adams's argument is her acknowledgment of the insufficiency of moral categories for describing the relation between God and persons. The persons we spoke with acknowledge that insufficiency. The conceptual inconsistency that lies at the root of the problem of theodicy is not lost on them, but they find other supramoral ways to think about themselves, their identity, and their relation to God. They inevitably wonder and worry about the issues at a conceptual level; it may be impossible not to. I want to explore ways of trying to comprehend the contradictions.

To this end it is helpful to distinguish two ways in which religious ideas might provide a context of meaning and support in the face of suffering and death. In one formulation, belief in a transcendent God puts tragic events in a broader context, and trust in God's sovereignty is comforting; in the second, God identifies with the sufferer and breaks the circle of isolation created by suffering and death. These ideas are fragmentary; they may be inconsistent with each other, but both the idea of the transcendent God and the idea of God identifying and suffering with us are parts of the Western monotheistic traditions.

God Is In Charge

Our respondents articulated the first of these themes more frequently, and more thoroughly, than the second. Speaking very broadly, the idea is that God, not the self, is in charge, and that fact is comforting. Some may think of a divine "plan"; for others, that may seem too facile. In any case the core idea is that because *God* is in charge somehow, in some sense, too much worry represents a grandiose sense of one's own importance and is inappropriate. The presence of the higher power is reassuring. For example, one "spiritual" nurse commented: "Part of what this job has taught me is that as humans we are so fragile. We can't do it all. And by nature, we try so hard to. And life is just so much bigger than us. And through watching patients go through dying and watching their families, there's definitely a source bigger than any of us that's in control." This "source" is spoken of with some modesty; we don't know much about it. But there is a sense of the reality of something that transcends normal objects and events.

How does this way of looking at things help? A Catholic physician said, "I don't know the answer to that. I just know the world is an awful big place, and lots of bad things happen, yet there is faith. T. S. Eliot, I think, says it best in 'East Coker' in his book, *Four Quartets*. Eliot talks about hope for the wrong thing. He talks about waiting without hope when hope would be hope for the wrong thing. Wait without thought, for thought would be thought for the wrong thing. But yet there is faith. And the love, the hope, and the faith are all in the waiting. So we have to wait and see. [In one case] the family was hoping for a miracle, and I suggested that they shouldn't lose hope, but maybe they were hoping for the wrong thing. Perhaps instead of hoping for a miracle, *what they should hope and pray for is that they can find the strength to accept what's happening.*"[4]

For these persons, belief in or loyalty to a transcendent God does not imply the likelihood of miraculous interventions. To be sure, unexpected things do happen, and who knows why? The key contribution of the relationship to God is simply that relationship itself. God's power and goodness are presumed, but not a lot more than that is known, or claimed to be known, about God. This form of piety sounds a strong note of acceptance, recognition of the inevitable, and a search for help in coping. With acceptance comes reassurance.

Thus one social worker said: "The most important lesson that I had was when I was a child and my grandmother lived with us. She had rheumatoid arthritis and was in a wheelchair. At night if I was helping her get to bed, we had a homemade bedside commode that she could use, and then she could slide over into her bed. I would need to lift her legs up into bed and cover her up. And I'd kiss her on the forehead and say, 'Night, Mammy. I'll see you in the morning.' And this very peaceful voice would say, 'The good Lord willing.' And it's like I'm not in charge of that, you know. Somebody else is in charge of that, and I'm okay with it. She had lived as well as she knew how to live, and she was not in charge of her death. That picture is still very strong in my mind. And I think that has helped me not to have a fear of death."

Acceptance need not translate into practical fatalism. For example, an evangelical nurse said: "'Lord, it's in your hands. This is what I'm going to do. If it's not what You want me to do, then You can change the course.' I'm not just sitting around waiting for things to come to me. I'm a mover and do things, but I commit it and say, you know, 'If this isn't what You want me to do, show me. Redirect me or something.'" Here acceptance is explicitly associated with resistance to suffering and death. In this case the formulation relates to the nurse's sense of calling. If God does not want her to be acting as a nurse, God might direct her into some other line of work or vocation. Acceptance of God's power or sovereignty never means that it is all right to allow people to suffer. As Max Weber pointed out years ago, a notion of God's sovereignty—far from inspiring passivity and quietism—may lead to dynamic action.[5] Feeling allied with God's purposes, the believer may feel especially empowered. Acceptance and action can go hand in hand.

The notion of surrender to God's sovereignty requires caution in our moral judgments. I asked one chaplain about an awful (and to me senseless) death that he had described. He responded, "What is a senseless death? Am I sure that's a senseless death? [I]f you don't believe things are the way they should be, you'll go crazy. For some reason, things had to be this way. I can no more tell you why some babies live seven days, and some babies live seventy years. It's not for me to know. I'm not God. I don't have to have all the answers. And that's really quite pleasant—that I don't have to have all the answers. All I have to do is have faith that God knows what God's doing with the universe. I don't know what a senseless death is. I remember a man who hanged himself. His wife had been in and out of a mental hospital for years. After the funeral, she got her GED, went to work in the hospital, became the head of the department, opened a store, opened a second store, opened a third store. She's now the happiest woman I've ever seen; his 'senseless' death [liberated her] from that awful marriage where he beat her on a regular basis, which nobody knew about because she never said anything. She always just checked herself into the hospital in an almost catatonic state. His senseless death gave her a brand new life. So I don't know. I can't be quick enough to judge what's a senseless and a meaningful death. Or, are there any *meaningful* deaths?"

Recognition of the sovereignty of God may lead to acceptance or activism, but it is always associated with a kind of letting go, a recognition of the limits of human power and responsibility. That brings sanity to many of these professionals. They have a kind of inner peace that comes with recognition of their limits.

God Identifies with Us

For one of our respondents, this confidence rested in a god imagined in highly personal terms. This evangelical physician talked about her son's serious illness. "I was really so angry with God. 'God, don't you know what it's like for me to have to see my son hurt like this? I'd cut off my arm, give my heart, I'd just do anything to stop my son's pain. You don't know what this is like. I know you can fix this, and I really am tired of you not fixing it. You know, I've just about had it with you.' And then I was brought up short, and I could say, 'Yeah, God, you *do* know. You *do* know what it's like to see your son, you know, just writhe in pain.' God let his son stay on the cross in pain, even though he could have fixed it, because he knew that we needed that escape. We needed that potential for salvation. And so he let his son hurt that much for my sake and for my son's sake. And at that point, I could say, 'Okay. God, if you can make good come out of my son's pain, it's okay. I'll live with it. Even if he never walks again, that's okay. I'll buy a wheelchair. I'll redo the house. I'll do whatever it takes if you can be glorified in my son's illness. Now, that's not to say I would like it. It's not to say that I wouldn't grieve like every other parent. But I could say, 'God, it's okay.' Of course, since God is in charge anyway, it's kind of a moot point. But I kind of said, 'Okay, God. I'll let you go ahead. You know, whatever you do, I'm willing to let you be in charge and just use me.' And that was a very peaceful thing. And I think I just thoroughly have enjoyed life even more than usual, more than the past, because I've had this tremendous peace. Whatever happens, it's okay. It's okay. So I do find a great deal of satisfaction in knowing that when people die, other than giving the family Valium, there is something I can do to help them make the best of this death. Because you can make good things out of death. Even the death of children, you know, can be okay. It's okay. If God lets it happen, it can be used for good."

This doctor has a highly anthropomorphic view of God, one many—including many of her fellow Christians—do not share. Her notion of a personal God weeping over the suffering of His Son is highly comforting to her. For her, God has suffered as any parent has suffered, so God understands. Of course, God not only understands, God is in charge. But God's Lordship or rule, which includes the suffering in the world, is not upsetting and can even be comforting, because God has shared the sufferer's experience. It is not so much God's power as God's involvement, the suffering ascribed to God as parent, that is important in the life of this physician.

While no other respondent articulated a similar view, several respondents reported finding support from a notion of God somewhat different from traditional or popular concepts. At least two recognize the importance of Rabbi Harold Kushner's book *When Bad Things Happen to Good People*. One said,

"Sometimes I find that I have trouble getting on the same wavelength if someone speaks in very traditional Christian terms. I'm just not able to enter into that because I don't think that I think of God as good and evil. Rabbi Kushner said it's not, 'God, why have you done this to me?' But 'Give me strength to help deal with whatever I have to deal with.' And it's more of a strength and support than, you know, of punishing." This comment amounts to a rejection of the highly personalized piety of the physician just cited; indeed, it's a rejection of any form of moralism; God is not imagined as good or evil. The issues transcend morality.

This leads to a different way of understanding God's assistance or support. One chaplain said, "I perhaps grew up like most people thinking that God was like that rough lucky rabbit's foot that kept bad things from happening to you. Rabbi Kushner's book, *When Bad Things Happen to Good People*, is a more mature expression of faith. To understand God as being that one who is with you in the midst of life's experiences, rather than the one who kind of picks you up and transports you out of life's experiences. Wraps you in some protective foil that keeps bad things from happening."

Kushner explicitly affirms the finitude of God. One of our chaplains remarked, "Well, I'm kind of a process theologian. And I think there are dangers in the world, and I don't think God rescues us from the dangers in the world. And I don't think God is rescued from the dangers in the world. Create a world like this, there are some dangers. Meaning in life does not exactly have to do with how pleasant your life is. As a matter of fact, more meaning has come out of suffering and pain than almost any other experience of humankind, seems to me."

This point about the suffering God could be articulated even more forcefully using some traditional categories. For example,

Jurgen Moltmann has argued that it is essential to acknowledge the crucifixion of God (i.e., the fact that God entirely identified with us in our suffering and death). His proposal is radical and sophisticated; he speaks of the God *event* rather than the being of God. The crucial point is one that has been central to Christian piety from the very beginning of the Christian movement: God is with us; God has identified Himself with us. In contrast to saying that God is a parent who is like us in His role as parent, this view suggests that God is like us in the fact that he identified with us and suffered with us as mortal people. Theological affirmation of that action implies that we are not alone in our suffering and death. Indeed as those we love suffer and die we are in community, or in communion, with God.[6]

I was frustrated by the fact that few, if any, of our respondents articulated this view because I think it is the core of the distinctively Christian response to the crises of suffering and death. Christianity is distinguished from its Abrahamic siblings Judaism and Islam by its claims about Jesus of Nazareth as the Christ, by the idea of the Incarnation of God in a person. Over the centuries Christians have shed as much religious heat as light over this claim, and it has been a highly political, as well as theological, point of controversy since before the Council of Nicea in 325 CE. But as a matter of practical piety, Christians should not lose track of the religious reason that the Athanasian party, and much of Christianity subsequently, wanted to affirm the full presence of God in the Christ: human salvation comes from identification with God.

The core idea is that salvation comes when people recognize that they are not alone. The Christ is a kind of Everyman whose suffering and death are followed by new life. We as Christ's "adopted children" or "spiritual heirs" may hope that our lives follow the same pattern. With God we each suffer pain and estrangement; then we have hope of some sort of resurrection. We are not alone in our suffering, and the notion of community or communion in suffering is religiously powerful. It provides suffering persons with a pattern and reference point, an intellectual precedent and context, for their suffering. It suggests a special kind of relationship to the eternal, a relationship that some of the early Fathers were willing to call divinization. It suggests that all human life, including the suffering that leads to death, has a sacred quality.

Theologically it is imperative to affirm that God identifies completely with humankind. Otherwise the story is simply a cosmic fantasy, rather than an insight into human reality. To the extent that that identification is incomplete or tentative, the core New Testament story becomes strictly a performance, only accidentally related to our suffering and fears. We didn't need that; we always knew we suffered. However, if the heart of the universe is with us, and there will be new life, we are broken out of isolation and given hope.

The key moral implication of God's identification with us in our suffering is the importance of replication on a smaller scale; it is at the level of human relations, not the level of conceptual analysis. As God was authentically present with us, so should we be authentically present with each other. My initial reaction of disappointment that our conversation partners did not more clearly state these ideas was academic and undiscerning. This is a theodicy of action and identification, not of ideas. The presence of another person can be an image of the presence of God.

Communal Support

Nurses, chaplains, and many physicians see the provision of special personal support as a key characteristic of their role, as mentioned in chapter 2. Just exactly what does it mean to provide personal presence? Margaret Mohrmann[7] argues that a crucial component is "a capacity to listen to the non-sense of suffering . . . because the intensity of suffering is often directly related to its degree of senselessness." So what does the professional say when someone asks, "Why me?" Mohrmann rejects answers such as "It's the luck of the draw" as overly fatalistic, and it seems to me that she is right. More particularly, an appeal to the impersonality of fate may fit with the notion of an inexplicable and transcendent God, but it fails to reflect human community or solidarity, identification with the sufferer. Those notions of community and identification require a response that is less distanced and more involved. What are the key characteristics of that response? For our respondents, they are listening, providing professional corroboration, and providing personal engagement.

Mohrmann argues that professionals can make God present to another through a threefold process that begins with "receiving the patient's story." This entails listening to the patient talk about his life and fears and hopes, reflecting on what's said, and reviewing it with the patient. Something like this process of listening, reflection, and review seems to capture what our respondents talk about in terms of providing presence. Mohrmann goes on to suggest that listeners should not be too quick to absolve the patient from a desire to take responsibility for what has happened to her or her loved ones. Listening, she notes, means treating someone's story as authentic, even if the story seems destructive, and being present may mean attempting to offer a reordering, a revision of the story. But the key and initial step is listening, internalizing, and signaling that one has heard. As I validate the story by listening, I provide identification and community for the other.

Mohrmann's insight is corroborated by our conversations. One chaplain remarked that his experience with a dying woman early in his ministry taught him "the importance of listening, of presence. There were days when I would go to her room, and it would be a bad day for her. And I would say, 'This may not be a good day to talk.' And she would shake her head. And I would say, 'Would it be better if I come back another time?' And she would shake her head—No—again. And I would say, 'Would you like me to just sit?' And she would affirm that. And so I would sit for ten, fifteen minutes, maybe twenty, depending on whether my pager went off or not. (I learned how much I hated those old voice pagers that we had in those days, which interrupted a time that was quiet.) It was awfully hard for me, initially, to do that. But I learned the importance of sitting quietly and not saying anything. And what appears to us often as not *doing* anything. We want to *do* something."

When asked about the worst thing that a chaplain can do in caring for a dying patient, another chaplain responded that the worst thing was being part of a conspiracy of denial. He added, "Giving advice. We all have a tendency to use clichés and give advice and make judgments. I guess clergy, particularly, are pretty good at those things. And yet, those are precisely what you don't need. You don't need anybody giving a sermon at that time, and you don't need anybody making judgments. I think those are pretty major no-no's. The main thing that they should be doing is just being there silently and supportively and being available to the people and helping them. Facilitating their decisions and their thinking processes. But mostly you do that by silence and by touch. Just doing caring kind of things without saying a word. But that is the hardest part, because it's difficult to be quiet. And you feel like you are wise to say something."

Many of our respondents think that the need to talk about presence is a sad commentary on their profession and stress the importance of presence *by the professional*. The loneliness and alienation experienced by the dying is a central theme of Leo Tolstoy's great novella *The Death of Ivan Illych*, where the key personal presence is provided by a servant. That is a role professionals should be willing to play. Sometimes their presence may be needed because the professional can reassure those involved that what is going on is normal and predictable, even if sad and unwanted. Asked what dying patients and families expect from health care providers, one nurse said, "I think comfort and just being there to support them. You tell them about how the breathing is going to change. You talk about the 'old-fashioned death rattle,' as they call it. You know, you hear that gurgle, gurgle, gurgle. And you go through it with the family and say, 'Now, you're going to hear this,' and you're going to hear, 'Can't we just suction that out?' And we go through that over and over and over. 'No, we can't.' And it never fails. So I think it's just being there, reinforcing one more time. Even though patients want to die at home, and families want to grant that wish, they need professional personnel with them just to say, 'Okay. I'm doing okay.' I think they feel that maybe they could do one more thing. But if a professional is there saying, 'No, you're doing good. You're doing okay.' Then it's okay, you know. So I think support is really the issue and the reinforcement of 'You're doing okay.'"

Presence may be important even if the practical result is failure. "One of our hospice patients was a very difficult patient [with whom] to establish pain control. And his terminal day, both a hospice nurse and I were present and were [unsuccessfully] increasing his morphine trying to obtain some comfort. [Afterwards] the family was just glowing with praise at what a wonderful death this had been. That's an example of how one's presence is so much of what's needed." Despite failure in their own eyes, these professionals helped enormously by being present *as* professionals. Their knowledge and experience make their presence particularly important even if their skills don't work.

Some time may have to pass before presence is really appreciated. As one nurse commented, "There are some families who operate a lot on information and data. And I've experienced that professionally with families. I have found that once you have given them that and they realize that there is no other place to go except be here, then it is a matter of presence and just being with them." In effect the gift of presence may be offered from the beginning, but patience is called for in the interval before it is accepted—if it ever is.

Presence is not just passive but includes engagement of the self. Asked about the values he'd like to pass along to doctors in training, one physician said, "Respect the dignity of your patients. Communicate with them. Don't be afraid to give of yourself to these patients, because that's what they want. They don't always want the answers; they want the support. They want to see us human. They want to see you struggle with their death. Listen to their pain. Listen to their families. Watch people die. Learn what is a good death and bad death, according to your own definition. And apply that to your own practice." At a minimum this formulation seems to require communicating a sense of caring, letting some emotional involvement show. It requires a degree of empathetic identification with the patient and speaking in the language of "we" to signal steadfast support to the end.

One chaplain remembered a PBS video called *On the Edge of Being*. It comprised interviews with six dying patients; one was a physician who offered a "critique of his colleagues, who were caring for him. He said, 'You know, what I expect from you is that you hear my questions. I *know* that you don't have the answers. I know that I have questions to which *nobody* has the answer. But struggling with me, with my questions, you show me respect. You *value* me by listening to my questions.' And that was very profound." Those present are expected to grasp what the questions are, to appreciate the questions on a cognitive level; but that doesn't mean they are expected to answer them. There is an intellectual component to presence, but it isn't having the answers.

And, as I suggested, there is an emotional component. I asked a respondent, "What do you think is the most important thing a nurse should bring to the care of the dying patient?" She said, "I think the nurse needs to bring presence. The failing would be presence without compassion, but that's not really right. Sometimes nurses are too afraid when they're asked by family members or patients to give their honest feelings. And they'll just say, 'No, you need to ask the doctor that.' I think most nurses who have gone into oncology go to it knowing that that's part of what they have to do and are generally pretty good at it. That doesn't mean every single one of them is, but most of them are. They're good with families. They're there. They cry. And all of those things. Particularly with patients who we end up keeping for long periods of time, and we become their family. Many of our nurses attend funerals and callings."

Our professionals were aware that the support relationship runs both ways. Professionals get support from patients. One evangelical physician was surprised at the level of support she received when her family dealt with serious illness. It was, she says, "a very, very satisfying period of time. [Partly because of] the outpouring of people to me. I'm always in the business of 'What do you want me to do for you?' And nine times out of ten, people want something from me. But in this situation there really were people who wanted to give to me."

A Catholic doctor said, "I often question myself after a gut-wrenching day of spending time with people in the operating room and say, 'How could God let this happen?' and 'What did this person do to deserve this?' But I have also had those people teach me to have a perspective on that, too. Their process of dealing with it has been educational to me. It has comforted me in some ways [and] it's taught me what is important in my life. And you know, just when I think that I have troubles or I'm worried about something or I'm concerned or I'm angry about something, I focus in on what happened to me that day or that week, about what someone else's burdens are that they are bearing, whatever cross they are carrying. And think about my own cross and think of it in comparison to that."

As a practical matter, the most deeply religious response to inexplicable and tragic suffering and death is the creation of community; explaining that is just what's required of a sound theology. This community is open to anyone who may suffer and die. And it may extend beyond the grave.

Afterlife

Several of the evangelical nurses we interviewed are clearly helped by a traditional belief in life after death. For example, asked if she believed in an afterlife, one nurse said, "Sometimes I wonder how people live day by day without God in their life. I mean, if you . . . look at people that don't, or you take care of patients that don't, you just wonder, how do they look at their future or their death, if they don't have any hope in afterlife?"

But the evangelicals aren't alone. Asked if she believed in an afterlife, a spiritual nurse said, "Oh, absolutely. I don't know that I have a real handle on what I see as the afterlife. But having seen patients die, been at the bedside of patients dying, there is something that leaves. It's blatantly obvious to me that something leaves. One of the [other nurses who] had been an oncology nurse for many years said after she was at her father's deathbed, 'You know, all the times of being at somebody's bedside and not knowing, really, what I believed—but being there *something* happened.' She said, 'I'm not sure I know what it is, but I know my dad is okay. As much as it hurt me for him to be gone, I knew he would always be with me. He was there with me somehow, somewhere, something like that.' And she's not religious. She's not a person who has a faith, wasn't raised in the church or anything. I believe in God. I believe that there is a higher power. I think that there's no way that we could be on this earth and the human body be the way it is without there being some other kind of power to make it work that way. To work the way that it works. Or that people could come up with the things that we've come up with to care for people. I think the human body is the most amazing thing imaginable, and that's all it is, is a house. And that once the soul is gone, then the house is no longer of use."

The same point about ongoing contact was made by one Catholic nurse, who reported, "In fact, I feel sometimes I'm closer to my father in his death, in his not being here, than I was during his life. Because I feel like there is a communication, because it's a communication of spirit. Now again, how do you scientifically prove that? You don't. It's a matter of faith."

Or a chaplain: "I believe that when this life is over, we go somewhere. I'll be happy to see what God has in store for us. You cannot work with the dying very long without believing—[or see] a dead body, after the person has died *without* believing—that that spirit has gone somewhere. I'm using very vague terms because that way it covers more ground. I work with nurses who are agnostics and atheists, who believe in an afterlife. Which is astounding to me, but just because when a person dies, it's a holy and sacred moment."

Belief in an afterlife is not always comforting, as another chaplain noted. "My own theological journey is coming from a very fundamentalist, conservative position and moving to a different position—in comparison to where my father and my mother are, a very liberal position. The way my working with death has played into that has to do not so much the death itself but with afterlife. What if my dad is right? I don't think he is. But what if he is? We'll all go to hell. I don't even believe in hell anymore. But that's where I'll be going, if he's right. And I carry that fear. I cannot escape that fear, so existentially it's always with me. What if he's right? What if those guys on TV are right? What if God really isn't totally graceful, unconditional in God's love for me?"

More typically, however, another chaplain said that his work has changed the way he looks at death. "Not that I'm any less afraid of death or any less apprehensive about death, but I've seen so many people die. And I don't think the moment of death is a particularly bad time. Sometimes getting there can be terrible, but that's what we fear. It's not that moment of death but that period of time between. I have a kind of a deep faith that God does preserve, [and] restore life, or maybe beyond life; I have a kind of sense that God will take care of me at the end of my life. And basically I think that's okay. That's good."

Certainly none of these responses amount to a proof of the immortality of the soul, or of the existence of life after death. Few, if any, of our respondents could say with any confidence what they expect after death. These comments reflect a considerable diversity of perspectives. What is striking to an observer whose home is the secular university is the frequency and conviction with which many of them voice the belief that someone's story does not end at death. This group of people is not unfamiliar with the biological facts of death; and their affirmations are modest and diverse. But their tentativeness is combined with conviction. Moreover, this belief is something that several respondents volunteered. We did not include an explicit question on life after death in our inter-view schedule.

Conclusion

At the end of the day, the most that can be said is that we have fragments of a response to the tragic character of the endings of many lives. One fragment involves affirmation of a transcendent God—trusting in that God and seeing our moral judgments and fate as of less than ultimate importance. An-other fragment of response affirms God's identification with us in our suffering and demands that we be companions with each other. Yet a third affirms an ongoing presence of self af-ter death.

These fragmentary, perhaps inconsistent, responses amount to a kind of practical theodicy, a set of partial perspectives on the world of care for the dying. We'll next turn to a specific is-sue of contemporary moral controversy to see how these frag-mentary perspectives may structure thinking about it.

Notes

1. Margaret E. Mohrmann, "Someone Is Always Playing Job," in *Pain Seeking Understanding*, ed. Margaret E. Mohrmann and Mark J. Hanson (Cleveland: The Pilgrim Press, 1999), 69.

2. Marilyn McCord Adams, *Horrendous Evils and the Goodness of God* (Ithaca, N.Y.: Cornell University Press, 1999).

3. Adams, *Horrendous Evils*, 82–83.

4. Emphasis added.

5. Max Weber, *The Protestant Ethic and the Spirit of Capitalism*, translated by Talcott Parsons (New York: Charles Scribner's Sons, 1958).

6. Jurgen Moltmann, *The Crucified God: The Cross of Christ as the Foundation and Criticism of Christian Theology* (London: SCM Press, 1974).

7. Mohrmann, "Someone Is Always Playing Job."

CHAPTER FOUR

~

Deciding for Death

Introduction

Much of the bioethical discussion about end-of-life care focuses on the question of which forms of care should be permissible or prohibited. For the past decade, the focal point in that discussion has been the question of physician-assisted suicide (PAS), which was legalized in 1997 in Oregon. I want to make three points about what I have learned from conversations with physicians, nurses, social workers, and chaplains and what I think it's important to focus on. First, they are ambivalent about legalization; they think legalization is unnecessary, and that it may lead to abuse. Second, on the basis of what they had to say I conclude that for them, it is not an ordinary moral issue; it is a religious or spiritual issue as well. The stakes are higher here than in ordinary moral quandaries. Third, I will spell out the implications of seeing the issue of physician-assisted suicide through the partial theodicies that focus on God's transcendence or God's presence with us.

How Our Respondents See PAS

Ambivalence

In our interviews we heard a lot of ambivalence about physician-assisted suicide. For example, when asked if he favored physician-assisted suicide, one chaplain responded, "That's like saying, 'Do you still beat your wife?' There should be a decent way to get out of this world without having to hang around for the last gasp. Because there are a lot of . . . times we save people from easy deaths to die worse deaths later on." He added that "as far as giving somebody medicine to put them away . . . [I]f you had a beloved pet, a cocker spaniel, who was in a great deal of pain and agony and could not get well, and every moment brought them more pain and agony, you would take them to the vet, and the vet would put them out of their misery. Why should we not treat a beloved grandparent just as well as a cocker spaniel?"

In content, if not in form, that's a rather typical chaplain's response. Our chaplains are not overly concerned with the letter of the law. In contrast, one nurse, said, "No. I don't [support PAS]. It's just an ethical thing with me. I guess I believe everybody has the right to do what they choose, but not for me. I could not do that. I believe there is a God . . . and I go back to that scripture in Ecclesiastes . . . that says something about there's a time to be born and a time to die." This response again is similar to that of her fellow nurses. This nurse clearly sees why someone might request or consider performing PAS; she is ambivalent in that sense. But at the end of the day she is clear about her opposition.

A physician responded with complete candor when asked, "Do you support physician-assisted suicide?" "I do not. I'm not sure why I don't, but I just don't." Another, generally opposed to PAS, says, "I don't know how I would personally be if I knew I had a terminal illness, having excruciating pain or debilitation, if I would commit suicide. I would like to think I wouldn't, but I guess one of the things as I approach fifty is I've become far less judgmental. I know so many circumstances in life where until you actually are in that position, you can be as theoretical and as high and mighty and as principled as you want to be. But who knows what the thought is going through each person's mind? What things are not resolved? What things are priorities? But I have a very difficult personal philosophy with dealing with physician-assisted suicide."

PAS Is Unnecessary

Because they believe that pain can be controlled, the people we talked to are not persuaded by arguments from the possibility of uncontrolled pain. One nurse said that she doesn't support PAS "because I think that you *can* manage pain. . . . [I]f you just try hard enough and try different things, you can do it. A lot of people think morphine is the only answer, and it's not. I mean, you can do spinal kinds of things; you can block nerves. If somebody is going to die anyway, what's the big deal of blocking a nerve? I mean, they may choose to not be able to feel their toe in order to be pain free. I think we need to let them make that decision. And we tend not to do that. So I don't think assisted suicide is okay. And part of that is my religious beliefs, that I don't think it's okay. But I also don't think it's necessary."

Because their responses presuppose a social and technological context in which pain can be controlled, we cannot guess what these professionals would think about difficult deaths in times and places where effective pain control was (or is) not possible. Some of them appeal to religious or other principles that might yield a universal prohibition on PAS, whatever the consequences, but they see the professional world in which they work as one in which a possible conflict between absolute principle and alleviation of suffering is minimized.

Abuse and Disrespect

An additional cluster of reasons our respondents' resist physician-assisted suicide is the perceived likelihood of abuse and injustice. For example, a chaplain who is among the most liberal on this issue insists on the need to be certain "that [the request] is not a financial thing . . . [made] because they feel they don't have the money to proceed with the treatments or stuff like that." This man might agree with Max Mehlman[1] that dying to save money is not intrinsically corrupt, but he is vividly aware that persons with adequate financial resources or good insurance plans have better options than those who lack those assets. Some people are much more likely to feel financial pressure to die than others.

These professionals fear that patients may make unnecessary and premature choices for PAS; in the real world of health care, they fear that it will become an engine of injustice. "[I]f every patient had access to a hospice program, and there were no barriers—they had access physically, financially and so forth—I would be hard put to say that there are not cases that one would seriously consider helping a patient end their life. But [it's different] . . . in the context of our current access to care and all of the ramifications that might make a patient feel obliged [to end his/her life]." One dimension of the issue is overt lack of access to curative or palliative care, a deficiency that may make resignation from life more attractive to persons in tight circumstances. One empirical study found that patients who had "substantial care needs were more likely to report that they had a subjective sense of economic burden . . . and that they or their families had to take out a loan or mortgage, spend their savings, or obtain an additional job. . . . Patients with substantial care needs were more likely to consider euthanasia or physician-assisted suicide. Caregivers of these patients were more likely to have depressive symptoms

. . . and to report that caring for the patients interfered with their lives."

General Rules and Particular Exceptions

The vast majority, if not all, of these professionals prefer to see physician-assisted suicide ruled out by one or more policies or laws. Many respondents suggest a difference between moral standards that take the form of general rules or policies and those that should be used in assessing individual actions. They distinguish between policy, on the one hand, and their judgments about individual acts, or the character of individual actors, on the other.[2] Thus, after stating his opposition to the legalization of PAS, one chaplain said, "There are cases when I could in no way pass judgment on either a patient who desired that and resorted to that or a physician who assisted with that. There are situations that are so ambivalent that to know the absolute truth of that situation is impossible. . . . I do not support suffering, unnecessary, intractable suffering."

Another chaplain asserted, "I think if you do it, you ought to be risking everything to do it. The thing that Kevorkian does. . . . You give him a call, and you go up, and he helps you do it. I think that's just ludicrous in a way, because it does not bear the weight of the moment of death for him or for the people involved in it. I think it's trivializing life. I stood with a physician who tried to kill a patient one night. And he was sweating. He came out and he said, 'Chaplain, I don't know. What do I do? I tried to kill her, and I can't even kill her.' And the family was saying, 'Please end the suffering.'

"She died the next day. But I think your hands *ought* to be sweating. You ought to have thought through this very, very carefully. And you ought to have the full weight of moral responsibility on you when you do it, if it is ever done. I've seen several situations where I think it probably should be done, but I don't like the idea of legalizing it."

A physician said, "I've generally spoken out against both assisted suicide and euthanasia. I think that there are perhaps rare cases that would make bad law and policy, where it would be reasonable to honor patients' request to end their lives. There are a few cases I have come across lately. There might be one in a hundred of dying patients whose symptoms you can't control very well. Who don't ask to be killed, necessarily. They ask you to control their symptoms. But try as you might, you still can't do a very good job. And should one of those patients ask, 'Doc, you're doing your best to control the symptoms, but this isn't working, and I would just like to end it now.' I think that would probably be a reasonable request." Similarly, the physician who is clearest about the risks of legalizing PAS continues, "[Even in the context of our unjust system] there are some scenarios that one could come up with that might be difficult for me not to agree that probably it is best for the patient to end their life." The reason these physicians can support a legal prohibition on PAS is that they assume they will continue to be able to respond carefully to these requests.

Clarifying Responsibility

Some of the people we talked to explained how they would handle hard cases, such as the one just described, using the traditional Catholic analysis of action. They make use of some version of the rule of double effect, the claim that when the effects of an act are multiple (doubled), the actor is more responsible for some of those effects than for others. We found our respondents using some of this language. For example, a chaplain remarked, "We should not expect our doctors to intentionally hasten or instigate death. I think there is a difference between withholding and withdrawing treatment and killing the patient. . . . I can't think of situations in which the physician doing that would be understandable or even excusable morally." One physician said, "It's my job to control pain, and I will control pain. But I will not assist in any kind of suicide. . . . Now if there is a legitimate side effect of a medicine, and I know it will suppress his respiration, may or may not hurry his death, [then] I'll treat the pain. And I'll pay for the side effect, whether that's worsening of his condition, whether or not that's death. I'll accept that as a necessity of controlling the pain. But to specifically choose a therapy with the intent of killing someone, I won't do it."

A social worker said that she did not support PAS because "as a medical team, we have the responsibility to keep people comfortable, but I don't think we have the right to help them take their own life. And it's more of a religious point for me. I have no problem with it if you're trying to increase morphine and a side effect of that is that it may decrease the respirations, and then you titrate that morphine all you need. But if somebody's comfortable, you don't just give them a boost of that [in order] to make their life shorter."

Focusing on Religious or Spiritual Perspectives

To summarize what I have said so far: The professionals we interviewed are deeply ambivalent about the practice of physician-assisted suicide. They don't like the idea of defending killing as a general rule, but they want to respect patient choice and they oppose suffering. In their experience, PAS is rarely if ever necessary in order to alleviate pain; the practice could be disrespectful; and if it is ever justified it would have to be as a kind of "teleological suspension of the ethical." In general our nurses, the people who spend the most time with the patients, are the most consistently opposed to PAS; the MDs, who may be the most secularized, are more willing to think about it; and the chaplains, for many of whom taboos have been smashed or are seen as more malleable, are the most liberal.

This complex set of attitudes and judgments suggests that there is a widespread feeling among these professionals that taking human life raises issues that go beyond ordinary morality. Killing is a religious or spiritual issue as well as a moral issue. If I take someone's life, a boundary of a special, perhaps sacred, character has been crossed. It is natural for these professionals to consider the question of PAS within their religious or spiritual frameworks. No perspective, framework, or angle of vision that doesn't take the religious or spiritual dimension of the issue into account can possibly be adequate in conversation with them. So I will conclude this chapter by explaining what seem to me to be the implications of taking these religious and spiritual perspectives into account.

Religion and Decisions about Death

What difference does it make if we acknowledge the religious dimension of the issue of PAS? I want to suggest several components:

1. A framework of meaning, however fragmentary, affects the standpoint from which one sees the issue of PAS.
In a provocative essay Margaret Pabst Battin argues that we may be on the verge of a major cultural shift in our attitude toward death. Because of changes in the cause of death, religious attitudes, and increasing respect for individual rights, we may be coming to accept an ideal of "directed dying" in which "dying is no longer *something that happens to you* but *something you do*." This is a shift from an "enmeshed" to a more "dis-

tanced" perspective in which someone might find it rational to trade a few months of life for a better death. Battin wants us to adopt the "distanced" perspective and accept control over our own dying as we do control over our reproduction; for adherents to this position, setting a date for one's death would be a moral and cultural advance.[3]

Battin's use of the contrast between an enmeshed and a distanced ethic maps onto the theodicies of God's transcendence and engagement that I discussed in the previous chapter. The caregivers with whom we spoke are willing to venture some generalizations, as we have seen, but their primary touchstone is daily experience with persons who are seriously ill or dying. They feel that their experience does not fit with the proposed practice of PAS. They are certainly enmeshed. On the other hand, they sometimes take comfort in looking at things from the distanced perspective, from recognition that they are finite and not responsible for everything. They don't think they should act like God, empowered to decide just when to end their lives—the implication Battin herself draws from the use of the distanced perspective. Rather, the availability of the perspective is for them a source of consolation.

2. Acknowledgment of the sacred leads to a distinctive diagnosis of the problem.

For our respondents, actually confronting requests for physician-assisted suicide is rare; what is recurrent is seeing or hearing about deaths that are needlessly uncomfortable, protracted, and painful. Preoccupation with physician-assisted suicide, they think, is an off-target response to the current problems in care for the dying. The real problem is not the lack of a right to independent choice but rather a misplaced set of priorities in the provision of health care.

This point is important, for it illustrates the gulf between the moral world in which these professionals live and work and some of the philosophical proposals for legalization of PAS. In much of that reform literature, the key issue is patients' right to decide for themselves, and the driving force is a conviction that people should have that right. Efforts to restrict patient choice are condemned as paternalism. Thus, even if all deaths were comfortable, the compromised autonomy of patients who wish to choose for themselves would be reason to call for reform. Of course, objections to PAS might rest on other grounds, such as the possibility of abuse, but respect for individual rights and autonomous choice is a trump card.

The professionals we spoke to are very clear about the importance of patients' deciding for themselves, but they think the issue is more complicated than a denial of liberty. Asked about physician-assisted suicide, another physician says he considers the prominence of this issue to be "a marker of the failure of the medical system. I mean, there is no one whose pain cannot be controlled, even if it means making them comatose. . . . If someone is telling me, 'I'm suffering so much and I want to kill myself because of A, B, and C,' have I done my job to relieve their suffering to the degree that I can? Those patients are probably depressed. Many of them are lonely. Many of them are afraid, again, afraid of the unknown, afraid of the future, afraid of whatever people are afraid of. And I don't think we do a good job in our society of care for the dying."

Another doctor said "the plea for ending life is generally saying, 'Look, I'm afraid of being in pain. I'm afraid of losing control. I'm afraid my family will be devastated financially. I'm afraid of all of these things.' And if I hear that, I try to enter into a pretty extensive discussion of 'Why do you say that? What makes you say that?' We can be very good [at symptom control], and we can be better than we are, but we can't be 100 percent; there are a lot of psychosocial and spiritual problems that you simply can't cure. You can help. You can help to alleviate. But you can't always cure them." For him the really intractable problems are the "psychosocial and religious" ones, problems that surely compromise the kind of free decision making that legalization of PAS would theoretically confer (or increase).

One of our doctors said, "[A request for PAS is] not very common. One in 100, you might not be able to control their symptoms well. And then of the 10 in 1,000, maybe one of those would actually ask for assistance. And typically, if you control their symptoms, then the request goes away. So what I fear about the whole debate about assisted suicide and euthanasia is that it's kind of a lightning rod for the rights language. But in reality it's the wrong issue." The right issue is provision of comfort, support, and whatever spiritual counsel the patient may want.

3. Seeing the question of ending life within the context of a religious or spiritual framework affects one's prognosis or hope.

The professional perspective we encountered is informed by a different image of the self at the end of life than the model that is presupposed in the philosophical argument. These health care professionals see dying persons as caught up in biological and social processes that are and will remain largely outside their control. Whoever or whatever God may be, it is God (or the gods) that are in charge rather than they or their patients. The intrinsic limits on patients' powers to script their own lives or shape their own deaths are quite apparent to the people we interviewed. They are able to affirm diversity and support decisions different from the ones they themselves might make. They will go to great lengths to assist people in making their last days what the patients and families want them to be. However, they see clearly that those choices are constrained by disease or trauma, and they think that the highest priority should be easing those constraints as much as possible. In that sense insisting on approval of physician-assisted suicide seems to them an unfortunate distraction, a changing of the subject away from serious structural, institutional, and professional practice issues.

Thus, if they were to write a prescription for social reform, the respondents would probably want more responsive and better-trained professionals, alert to the availability of adequate pain-control measures. They would want family members and patients who are better prepared for issues at the end of life. To them, those educational and cultural changes are much more important than legalization of physician-assisted suicide.

4. Communal support is required when dealing with impending death.

The religious meaning frameworks all presuppose human limit; they advocate solidarity either as fellow mortals or caregivers. They make human vulnerability salient. The professionals themselves worry about patients and psychological pressure or social expectations. For example, if "your mother is in this situation [i.e., dying badly in a society with legal PAS] and whether you verbalize it or it's simply the implied thing, she knows she can ask for it. It's a lot of pressure on the dying person to walk out on the ice floe." As the theological ethicist Allen Verhey writes, "When we provide social legitimation of the option of suicide, we may increase options [on the menu], but we also effectively eliminate an option, namely staying alive without having to justify one's existence . . . . [O]ne may choose, of course, not to be killed, but the person who makes that choice is now responsible for it, accountable for living, and he or she can be asked to justify that choice."[4] Verhey finds this shift in the burden of proof highly troubling.

The powerless and the victims of discrimination are particularly likely targets of pressure to justify their continued existence. Minorities are historically among those groups. "Physicians may be too quick to interpret ambivalent statements . . . as pleas to die, because at an unconscious level they perceive the patient as not deserving. . . . Patients may have absorbed the negative messages that society has heaped upon them and perceive themselves to be unworthy of the efforts that might be needed to prolong their treatment or provide them with palliative treatment."[5]

Validating the religious dimension of medical decisions at the end of life suggests that proposed legalization of PAS be related not to an imaginary world of ideal secure decision maker but to the actual world of health care provision—a world that reflects the biases, injustices, and inequities of the larger society. The professionals I spoke with are concerned that legitimizing the power to end life will further undermine trust among the vulnerable, will be used unjustly, and will establish a social practice that will impose subtle—and not always subtle—pressure on persons to decide to resign from life when they are no longer "useful." Without a just and genuine community, the possibility of PAS is highly troubling. Restrictions are necessary in a real world of injustice and bias.

5. Religious frameworks of meaning focus on responsibility, on clarity about what someone is responsible for and the limits on his or her moral liability, but limited liability goes hand in hand with recognizing limited options for action.
I mentioned that some of our respondents used the "rule of double-effect" in explaining their view; the meaning fragments we are considering make using that distinction or something like it unavoidable. On the one hand, the professionals tend to oppose PAS for a variety of stated reasons that may or

may not be overtly religious. On the other hand, their professional ethic commits them to the care of individual patients,
and care entails the relief of suffering. The imperative to relieve suffering will trump everything, or almost everything,
else. Thus when they think about policy as citizens—perhaps
using a perspective that finds comfort in transcendence—they
oppose legalization. But when as clinicians, enmeshed and engaged in the struggle with suffering, they think about their patients, and they can easily imagine circumstances that might
lead them to stretch the rules. We should be troubled if caregivers did not feel this tension.

The core notion in the rule of double effect is that the way
to reconcile this tension, at least in part, is to try very hard to
offer accurate moral descriptions of our actions. Why? Because
every comfort-providing action that society considers an act of
killing reduces the number of morally legitimate options available as we try to combat pain and suffering. In the discussion of
care for the dying, the usual use of this rule is to justify administration of high levels of analgesia or sedation, even though
those drugs may depress respiration or heartbeat or shorten life
in other ways. Administration of opioid doses sufficient to relieve pain is distinguished from administration of an unequivocally lethal dose of the same or some other drug.

The standard distanced ethic critique of this strategy is to focus on consequences and to claim that acts with the same consequence must be essentially the same act. Thus if we know
that someone gave a patient an injection of a very heavy dose
of morphine and that he died, we know that the persons involved in giving the injection did something wrong—perhaps
murder. Christine Cassel, who holds this view, writes that "The
discontinuation of food and water leads inevitably to death, so
it is illogical to say that one's intention is not to make death
happen."[6]

If *intention* simply means "what the doctor knew would happen," Cassel is right. But if *intention* includes reference to motivation and context, she is almost certainly wrong. We frequently distinguish the things we know will happen as a result of our actions from the things we intend. A pitcher who is trying to strike out a batter intends just that; he doesn't intend the batter's consequent rage or property destruction when the hitter returns to the dugout. An awaited family member who speaks gently to a dying patient, thus allowing the patient to relax and die, does not intend that death, although he knowingly enables—perhaps causes—it. Producing accurate evaluative descriptions is in fact a matter of art and discernment.

To be sure, there is a real possibility of self-deception in this enterprise. People are not free to re-describe their actions in any way that is morally comforting to themselves. And possible disingenuousness is understandably troubling to thoughtful persons. For example, a nurse says, "I don't know what could happen to me for this, but I think we already do . . . [PAS] in a way. We keep people comfortable. We give them high doses of pain medicine. We're not actually giving them a dose that we know that's going to kill them. But there's not a nurse that hasn't given a shot of pain medicine, and the patient dies twenty minutes later, and we think, 'Oh!' . . . . But I think if you are keeping someone comfortable enough that you are kind of assisting them to die comfortably. Although you're not going over the edge and giving them the dose that you know is going to kill them." She continued, "We're in America, and all this freedom of speech and freedom of this and freedom of that. Why should they not have the freedom to die?"

This nurse comes pretty close to saying, with Cassel, that any acts that in some sense "cause" death must be morally described in the same way. But that is mistaken, and in fact she qualifies her assertions. She wants to be honest, yet she sees that there's a difference here, if only "in a way."

I believe this issue of careful act description is so vexed precisely because of the sacral power of death,[7] our inevitable preoccupation with it and ambivalence before it. Many of us have a great, and understandable, tendency to assume that whenever death is a consequence of an action, then the death either was clearly intended or it was opposed. Either I was trying to save the patient or I was trying to make him die. But there is a third possibility: that I am trying to make the patient comfortable, and whether he dies sooner or later is a secondary matter as I make my decision.

Care-giving institutions need to develop the habit of working out subtle but honest descriptions of caring acts at the end of life. The issue is not learning to rationalize, but being willing to recognize differences in intention, persons, and context. Drawing these distinctions will require some significant community building on wards and across professional lines, as well as within group practices and professional groups. Failing that development, much loving care will be prohibited through broad-brush prohibitions.

6. General rules and exceptions.

Because generating honest and morally responsible distinctions is hard, it is particularly important to address the problems with the restrictive-rule, discretionary exception policy that several of our respondents favored. In a nutshell, the problem with the general rule/exception view is that it regards some moral principles or rules as imposed from without and contrasts those with the practical and humane demands of actual practice.

To explain I will begin by making the best possible case for restrictive policy but permissive practice. Social rules or practices, on this view, are justified in terms of some fundamental moral commitments, but those commitments are always general. We can imagine cases that these general rules or principles will lead us to treat awkwardly, if not cruelly. Therefore we must recognize the possibility of justified exceptions, departures from the norm. These exceptions represent conscientious objection to a generally reasonable policy. To assure that the exceptions really are justified, we maintain the strict sanctions and complement them with institutional policies of silence when individuals conscientiously decide to depart from them.

It's easy to see the limits of this formulation. On the one hand, it opens the door to considerable clandestine and freelance conscientious objection. If the difficult choices are completely private, there is no possibility of review, and inevitably there will be highly inconsistent use of the tolerated exception. On the other hand, the blanket condemnation of any action that *might* be construed as simply lethal has the effect of stifling serious professional discussion of options that should be weighed when patients are suffering. Honest agonized wrestling with difficult moral issues—circumstances when people may really learn something about the moral life—is cordoned off from serious discussion of policy. The possibility of peer support is ruled out, and the effect is to justify rigid and overly general policy mandates.

If, to the contrary, we agreed that all morality is rooted in our common life, it would be clear to us that the involved parties need to work together to specify the implications of their shared commitments. One of those is valuing life, even when impaired; another is providing comfort. Thus our first reaction to the poor physician who was unable to "kill" his patient should not be "Did he violate one of *their* rules?" Rather it should be to ask how he found himself in this situation in the first place; what were the comfort-providing options open to him; with whom had he talked about this situation? We should not immediately think of a rule and possible exception, but of the requirements of care and the ethos of a hospital and medical practice. Our first question should not be, "Did he *do* the right thing?" It should be, "With whom had he been able to talk over this issue? Whom had he listened to? Who will listen to and converse with him afterward?" Heavy morphine dosage may well have been appropriate, but solitary ad hoc decision making was not. In effect, this poor doctor was isolated, despite the chaplain's support, and the hospital and his colleagues learned nothing from the experience. Any possible development of institutional practice or precedent was, at best, clandestine.

The problem we face is our inability to specify a way to work out the meaning of the rule prohibiting killing in the contemporary context of end-of-life care. Giving up the rule altogether would be self-betrayal; failure to wrestle with the hard cases would be to pretend that the circumstances of dying have not changed. The rule of double effect gives us a helpful benchmark as we sort out our options in this situation of moral perplexity. But it isn't an answer to our questions; it's a way of formulating them. "How can we care and relieve suffering but not kill?" Medical communities, patients, and families have to work together on specifying what the best answer to that question is in their time and place. To be sure, there are some general answers: no injections of air embolisms; no refusal to use opioids. But the devil is in the details, and the details must be worked out together for specific situations. This specification is a social and communal process; it requires some form of discussion, trial and error, and feedback. Morally serious people face the difficult and unglamorous task of creating a community of moral inquiry within a hospital, group practice, local community, or profession.

7. Creating community to deal with suffering and death.

The upshot of these last two chapters is to insist on the remarkable practical importance of creating effective and supportive professional communities to provide end-of-life care. This goes beyond the usual stress, in any occupation, on the importance of a pleasant workplace environment. We have to remember what is going on in these professional communities.

In the previous chapter I said that finding meaning in the face of senseless death entailed creation of a community—among the professionals and to a degree between professionals and patients. In different ways both the meaning fragment that acknowledges transcendence and the meaning fragment that promotes engagement imply the need for community. But in this chapter we see even more starkly why creation of community is important: it is because caregiving communities have to take on some responsibility for deciding which forms of care are best described as acts of love and which amount to unjustified killing. Local and unit-specific communities have larger guidelines as they carry out this process. They should not be in the business of improvising without reference to a larger social consensus. But they do have to take responsibility for some difficult judgment calls, and that is hard to do if the caregiving community is fragmented or at each others' throats. I turn to the question of community in the next chapter.

Notes

1. Maxwell J. Mehlman, "Dying to Save Money: Economic Motives for Physician-Assisted Suicide," in *Alternatives to Physician-Assisted Suicide* (Bloomington, Ind.: Poynter Center, 2000), 22–39.

2. They did not make distinctions among those general standards. Some may be expressed in terms of hospital rules, others as state or federal laws, still others as the code of a profession.

3. Margaret Pabst Battin, "Physician-Assisted Suicide: Safe, Legal, Rare," in *Physician-assisted Suicide: Expanding the Debate*, ed. Margaret P. Battin et al. (New York: Routledge 1998), 63–72.

4. Allen Verhey, "Assisted Suicide and Euthanasia: A Biblical and Reformed Perspective," in *Must We Suffer Our Way to Death? Cultural and Theological Perspectives on Death by Choice*, ed. Edwin R. Dubose (Dallas: Southern Methodist University Press, 1996).

5. Patricia King and Leslie E. Wolf, "Lessons for Physician-Assisted Suicide from the African-American Experience" in *Physician-Assisted Suicide*, ed. Battin et al., 91–112.

6. Christine K. Cassel, "Physician Assistance at the End of Life: Rethinking the Bright Line," in *Must We Suffer Our Way to Death?*

7. William F. May, *The Patient's Ordeal* (Bloomington: Indiana University Press, 1991).

CHAPTER FIVE

~

Community and Compromise

So far I have described the substance of the conflict over physician-assisted suicide, as well as the strategies that may be employed in response to deaths that challenge the goodness of God or seem meaningless. The implication of both these discussions was to suggest the great importance of developing strong communities within the settings where care for the dying occurs. By a strong community I do not mean one in which everyone agrees on the "right" choice, the "right" philosophy of life, or the "right" theology. Rather, I mean a community in which disagreements are handled civilly, with love and concern. One contribution religion can make to care for the dying is enabling the creation of such communities.

Vital religious communities are seldom communities of dogmatic or conceptual unanimity. They are sustained by a common loyalty and common practices: good-faith disagreements should not rupture the community. All the disagreements that were reported to us concerned the question of when and on whose authority to shift the highest priority in forms of care from attempts to cure to provision of palliation and social and,

when indicated, spiritual support. When is it time to stop trying to keep someone alive? Whose judgment counts? How best
to handle the inevitable disagreements at this emotionally
wrenching time?

First a short litany of disagreements and frustrations:

Staff may become the target of patient anger. "What I find
exhausting is the people who are angry and unreasonable and
vicious because they're scared. They're people who have a lot
of other relationship problems and coping problems and probably chemical dependency problems, . . . they bring those mal-
adaptive behaviors to the hospital experience. Add the stress
of this experience and their loved one dying and they act out
here. [Y]ou look at what's normal in people's lives and how
dysfunctional that becomes when they transfer it to this environment and what a challenge it is for the staff to cope with
that," one nurse said. "So that's where I feel most exhausted,
most vulnerable to really make sure my skills are always there
and always alert and concentrating on how to do it best for
this family. Because it's those families that end up with the all
points bulletin out to the social worker. 'You've got to do
something. You got to fix this.'"

Families may be bitterly divided. A chaplain reported about
a woman who "had gotten terminally ill, and her family rallied
around to help. Her husband was not very helpful, and the
family discovered in the course of this illness that not only her
daughter but also several other children in the family had
been sexually abused by the father. They were so angry at this
man. He would not take care of her, so they had to take care
of her. And some anger at her also. I spent a lot of time with
the sister of the woman who was sick, just dealing with her
anger about that. They let the husband come in and visit her,
and they would try to leave while he was in. At the point at
which she was pretty close to death, she called her daughter

in. I was standing on one side of the bed and her daughter on the other side. She looked at her daughter, and she said, 'I want you to promise me you will forgive your father.' And the second time she said it to this little fourteen-year-old girl, who was standing over there with tears in her eyes, crying, I said, 'You can't ask her to do that. I can't let you ask her to do this.' The daughter just kind of slumped down in her chair at that point, and she quit making the request."

Patients may be intimidated by family members. "One was a gal that I took care of who had a bone marrow transplant. She was twenty-one years old, newly married; she and her husband were living with her parents because they couldn't afford to be living on their own. When she was admitted to the hospital, her *mother* wanted to make all decisions despite the fact that she was no longer a minor, and she and her husband legally could make any decisions they wanted to. She got to a point where she was on dialysis and not doing well. And she asked me one day if she could just say no to dialysis. 'You know, you have that option. That's your choice.' Her mother threw a huge fit. And the girl ended up being dialyzed. She died probably four or five days later, but in that four- or five-day period she just fell apart. The person who died was not the person who came in; she lost all of her spirit and her ability to fight. She could never talk with her mom about dying, because her mom was sure she was going to live. I wanted to be a patient advocate, to talk to her about the things she wanted to talk about. But her mom didn't want to have any of those discussions at all. So you had to ask her mom to leave, and that caused problems."

Disagreements among caregivers are not uncommon. "A number of physicians that I deal with have taken the Hippocratic Oath to do everything possible they can to sustain life. I find a strong denial of death on the part of physicians and an

unwillingness to yield to the inevitable. Surgeons are just no-
torious for their inability to deal straight with patients and
families around what they didn't accomplish, [although] they
like it when it's gone well. I recall not too long ago our hospital had a surgeon [who] came out and did a ten-minute spiel
with the family on all the things that he had done—and then
informed the wife at the end of ten minutes that they weren't
able to save her husband. 'Oh, you did this, and you were able
to do that.' And it was so self-serving. I just took the guy out
in the hall one-on-one, and I said, 'I don't ever want to hear
you string out a patient's family like you just did. Say that the
patient died. I'll take the work from there. But that was just
unconscionable for you to say how much you did before you
informed this woman. She was getting hope the whole time
from all the things you had done and you set her up.' The image of her turning and putting her head away from the physician and into the wall, not able to respond or talk to him any
further."

Disagreements between nurses and physicians are the stuff
of repeated comment. Many nurses report that they have few
conflicts with patients, families, or chaplains, but that problems with some physicians were common, "because they don't
sit down with the family and discuss that death may be soon
and ask, What are the family's wishes? And what are the patient's wishes? And that's what living wills are for. And they
don't even bring them up and discuss that. Well, if you're a
family physician or a patient's physician, why don't you discuss
that on a couple of your initial visits, although people don't
want to bring it up? Sometimes I think that physicians leave it
too late to discuss it. You may be at the bedside. You may be
in the hallway, and you're now telling this family that it looks
like they may die soon, and if they stop breathing, should we
put a tube in their throat? And if their heart stops, should we

beat on their chest? And they're too emotionally involved to make a rational decision. And it's like, 'Well, of course, we want you to do something.' But now this patient could end up on a ventilator for weeks, months, with no hope of recovery. The physician just leaves it too late. Often the nurses talk about it to the family, then they go to the physician and say, 'The family doesn't want them resuscitated if anything happens.' Whereas he should discuss that with [the family], and he should be the one that writes the order. Often nursing has to chase them down and point this out to them. Some physicians are good at it, and some seem to ignore it until the last minute." As we will see, this feeling of disapproval may take the form of diplomatic suggestions or the occasional verbal confrontation.

Another common scenario is for professionals to be ready to see the inevitability of death while families remain unwilling or unable to act accordingly. "I can remember one situation especially," said one chaplain. "Three physicians were involved—a cardiologist, a neurologist, and a nephrologist. They said, 'This person has three terminal illnesses. She is dying of her kidney disease and her heart disease, and her brain is never going to function again.' The family sat there and listened to that and said, 'That's okay. You are her doctor. It's your job to keep her alive.' It was like water off a duck's back. 'Do everything.' They were immune to reason and to logic. Keep Mother alive. Of course, who am I to say that if the tables were switched, I wouldn't be saying the same thing about my mother, because it's not a logical thing. It becomes an emotional thing. And often I suspect there is some guilt involved and some whatever dynamic. Again it's the textbook case that if the chaplain has done his job right, you'll help the daughter to sit down and review this relationship and get in touch with all these feelings and resolve all these conflicts. And sometimes that works. But this is not a perfect world. We're not perfect chaplains. Sometimes those conflicts never get resolved. Or we never know fully what has prompted this person to say, 'Keep on treating this person,' in what's obviously, at least to the physicians, a futile situation."

Loving and caring for everybody they encounter is difficult, if not impossible, for these professionals. For example, when asked how her faith helps her in her work, one nurse tersely observed that what she needed most regularly was "Forgiveness, the mercy of God. Because I'll meet some families and people that I just totally cannot comprehend how you would ever want to be too long with them in the room. And so, mercy and forgiveness and humility would play a big part."

Disagreements over Care and the Role of God

In the last chapters I described two different ways of finding meaning in the face of suffering and death—two fragmentary perspectives on daily tragedies. One of them entails stepping back, seeing things from a perspective that finds solace in a transcendent God being somehow "in charge." The core idea is the inevitable and recurrent character of suffering and death, combined with relief from ultimate responsibility because God is the one responsible; the professional's power is limited. The other perspective is more enmeshed in the ebb and flow of practical life. A distanced perspective may be retained, but the more driving psychological force is a willingness to engage oneself with the people who are dying and their loved ones. One loves and cares as one has been loved and cared for in one's own personal or spiritual life. Self-fulfillment comes from this engagement and commitment. Each of these perspectives is reflected in strategies for dealing with disagreement.

The most important thing to see in the citations that follow is that when disagreement occurs, the patient's interest—we'll come to the distinction between interest and preference later—is universally held to be sovereign. As the power of fate or God transcends their own power, so the professionals see that the patient's interest transcends any one person's formulation of it. They are very clear that their work is all about respecting and doing what is best for patients. As a chaplain remarked, "The issue of professionalism is that the patient's rights and the patient perspective [is the one that] takes precedence. [This contrasts with] a minister and a local congregation where the minister and the local church have an implicit or explicit authority around matters of doctrine and faith expression and perhaps even behavior. Chaplains do not serve with that same kind of authority."

Some risks to the patient's health may well be tolerated so as to respect the values he holds. "I don't want to pick on religions, but we had one situation one time with a fellow who was of the Pentecostal faith. And they came into his room, and they were standing him up when he shouldn't have been stood up, and they were hitting him and praying for him and stuff. And that was very hard for me, because I felt like they were compromising his care. But on the other hand, for him, that was his background. That was real important for him. And that's when you want to say, 'Put him *down*! What are you *doing*?' You know. But talking with him later, it made him feel better. And so that's tough. That's real tough."

When patients and family disagree, nurses often help the patient stand up to pressure. "I think of [a young guy's] ongoing battle with leukemia because his mom couldn't let go. He had made some comment earlier about how he was getting really tired. He wasn't one to talk a lot. He'd talk with me more than most, but he still was not a big communicator. One of the times when she was out of the room I said to him 'You know, you have the right to make the decision to not go through any more therapy.' He didn't have much of a response. I said, 'Are you afraid of dying?' And he said, 'No. I'm afraid of my mom. Of what it will do to my mom when I die.' We continued to talk; finally I said, 'Are you afraid of telling your mom you don't want to do anything else?' And he said, 'Yeah. I'm afraid that would just kill her.' And so we talked a little more—that it is his right and maybe there is a way to discuss this with her. And he finally said, 'Well, would you be there with me?' And so I helped initiate the discussion that then allowed me to back out from it. I've never been afraid when a patient says to me, 'I'm really tired of all this,' to say, 'You know, you have the right to say [you] don't want any more.'"

Or the patient's interest may be defended against other professionals, as when one consultant physician reports of attempted therapies being maintained when they are no longer helpful. "For example, [the patient] may still be getting some chemotherapy, may be getting parenteral nutrition. And in those instances, I would try to discuss with the [attending] physician, 'What are your goals here? And is this the patient's desire?' And sometimes as a result of that, they will back off of what they were doing. And sometimes they will slam the phone down and tell me to mind my own business."

Rarely but unfortunately, the patient may need defense against persons who are neither family nor immediate caregivers. One of our physicians found himself involved in a regional cause célèbre. "There are a lot of things that are very private between physician and patient, physician and family. The legal profession interfered tremendously. And I was so angry at a lot of that that I almost quit medicine. I resented having my patient being turned into a case or a cause. I remember when I was in her room for the final consultation to decide whether enough was enough. And it was really pretty easy, because I saw all her dolls on the wall. And I thought of my own daughter playing with her dolls. And I said, 'Well, what would I do if that was my daughter?' If that was my daughter at that point in time, I would have let her go. So we made the decision. But I was very angry at the interference by different parties, political and legal, for interfering with that sort of prime, direct patient-doctor relationship, or a patient-family relationship. Essentially they butted in and tried to take it over, but at the end of the day the judge's ruling was so eloquently put that it was just great."

Usually the professional thinks it's time to let go before the family does. "There are many times when I have wished that people could let go of the need for more curative therapy and maximize the quality of life through enrollment in the hospice program and not continue to choose to be beat up by strong medicine and horrible side effects. But I wouldn't interfere with a patient's choice. I keep coming back to the patient's fundamental right to choose." In fact, she said, "I think sometimes I have a harder time accepting the physicians' continuing to offer things. But the kind of institution we're in is where they really need to observe more patients on a certain therapy that is a new therapy to see how individual patients respond. The physicians don't push it, but if the patient says, 'Isn't there something else you can give me?' I wouldn't want the physician to lie and say there isn't."

More controversially, it is clear to these professionals that patients are sometimes mistaken about their best interests. If possible, the professionals will try to bring perception and reality into alignment. The issue may be a short-term thing. For example, a nurse remarked "We have to respect their decisions. We've had people simply refuse treatment. Young people that possibly have good survival rates. I had an eighteen-year-old once that came in my outpatient clinic and sat down for his chemotherapy treatment and said, 'I don't want this.' And his dad said, 'Be quiet. Take the medicine.' And Dad stepped out for a cigarette, thank goodness, and I just stopped and told the boy, 'I'm not going to do this to you if you don't want me to. I'm not going to try to talk you into it. This is your body. This is your life. It's your decision.' And we gave him time just to sit there and gave him a box of Kleenexes. And after about fifteen minutes, he said, 'It's okay. I can do it now.'"

Moreover, disagreements may be minimized by restricting patient choice. For example: "I did have a patient whose lungs were very severely compromised. She asked for a therapy she had heard about, which her oncologist here said he didn't feel he could give her, because her lungs were already in such bad shape that he really didn't think that this therapy should be given to her. He declined her offer [to be a subject]. She went to another cancer center here in the city, got that therapy, had a terrible several days in the hospital, was discharged from the hospital, went home and died five to ten minutes after she got through her front door. That was the patient's choice, but I respected the physician who declined to give her that therapy. That's the only case that I've encountered like that." There's no way around the fact that this patient's choice was limited in her own interest.

In particular, confronting a patient in denial can become very difficult. "That is the most frustrating part. We have a young mom right now. She's bargaining, and she will do anything to have her cancer go away. You know, 'I'll sleep on a hard, cold floor if God will just take this cancer away.' She has said things like that. And it's frustrating. Sometimes it's the patient. . . . On the next day we'll say, 'Give her to another nurse that will be fresh with this young person passing away.'

Because sometimes if you have somebody on your assignment repetitively, you do start to get impatient with them. You have to take another group of patients or step away from a really bad patient to give yourself a kind of a mental break. That's difficult. It's hard. You know, you try to explain that to them. And sometimes I just have to go along with them and let them keep hoping. You know, sometimes that's the best." This nurse is clear that the patient has got it wrong, but she realizes that in this case she has to go along.

Premature agreement with a patient can lead a professional to have extended feelings of regret and guilt, however. One physician remarked, "The case that comes to mind is an elderly man with an unresectable lung cancer, who was clearly going to die soon. When I put the question to him about the resuscitation, he said that he would want to be resuscitated, give it a shot. I didn't agree with it, thought that it wouldn't benefit him at all. And I was actually in a hurry. He wasn't my patient. I was just stopping in to see if I could be of assistance to one of my colleagues. But I said I would talk to the patient about the resuscitation issue. And when I did, I was surprised to get that answer. Rather than spend the necessary time with him to fully explore what it meant to do everything it took to resuscitate him in his current condition, I let it go. I thought he'd get home, and then I would have an opportunity to revisit it, because I had just met him. I thought I could talk to him at home in a different environment and have him come to an understanding. So the Do Not Resuscitate order did not get written. And sure enough he has a respiratory arrest before he leaves the hospital and they almost gave up. They tried. It was in the middle of the night, and for half an hour they worked on him, and just as they were about to give up, they got back a blood pressure and a heartbeat. They transferred him to the intensive care unit. I came in the next day and found him there. But his brain was gone. It was just awful. I just wanted to put my fist through the wall when I saw him in the ICU like that. And then we had conversations with the family, a very big family, a wife and thirteen kids. Some of the family had heard him say, 'I want you to resuscitate me.' It was kind of his last wish, and the family felt, 'By God, we're going to honor his last wish; a miracle might happen.' We got into a theological discussion, actually, about a miracle, about hope and about God. [He was] transferred to another hospital, where they also had an ethics consult and tried to talk to the family about DNR, limiting treatment, and they wouldn't hear about it. Then he finally died. After a full court press, he died. It was just awful. It was a very bad death." This physician clearly thinks that a patient may mistake his own best interests, and he feels an obligation to help the patient come to terms with reality. That is to say, he believes that the patient's interest transcends or is distinguishable from his own preferences or judgment.

Disagreement over patient interest may lead to confrontation between professionals and families. "I can remember one patient who certainly was an elderly person, had lived in a nursing home, and had very little quality of life. He was bedfast, had bed sores, and seemed unaware of any of his surroundings. His son insisted that everything be done, always, every time. And I did that a few times when he had pneumonia and brought him to the hospital with the expectation that if he quit breathing we would pound on his chest and do all those heroic measures. And then, having taken care of that man for a number of years, there [came] a point where I had to call the son and say, 'I can't do this. You know, it is not my belief [that this is] what your father would want. We're not providing any quality of life for him. And I just want you to know if I put him in the hospital, we can keep him comfortable but I'm not going to pound on his chest. I'm not going to shock his heart. I'm not going to put a tube down his throat to breathe for him. And if that's a problem for you, I understand, and I certainly can find you a doctor who can respect your wishes. But I feel like your father would not want me to do that.' And actually, he was okay with that. I certainly wanted to keep that up front. I didn't want to make that decision against his will, but I could no longer be a party of medical care that I felt was inappropriate. It was really inappropriate to continue to make that man live when all quality of life was gone."

It can also work the other way, with the professional thinking that life-sustaining treatment should continue. "[I remember] a case where hydration and nutrition became an issue and I withdrew my care from the patient and explained to the family that I couldn't participate, because I felt like they were starving someone to death, and I felt it was too early and that the dignity in the process of dying was being compromised. And for that purpose, I said, 'I would gladly get you another physician to care for your family member, but I have objections to it.' I was conflicted about that."

Disagreement over Patient Interest

These comments suggest several things. All the professionals are prepared to accept patient choice at the end of life, but they are pretty clear that some choices may lead to hardship for the patient. They want the patient to choose what is in his or her best interest, and that choice cannot be made if the patient hasn't recognized that life is coming to an end. Thus the professionals work with a sense that there is such a thing as the patient's best interest—something everyone concerned is trying to specify and act on as best they can. This best interest is, therefore, distinguishable from any one person's (patient, family member, caregiver's) conviction. It transcends convictions and perceptions. Of course all the various parties to the conversation believe that they know what that interest is; but the fact of good-faith disagreement shows that someone, perhaps everyone, is mistaken.

This recognition that there is something called the patient's interest reflects the "God's in charge" or limited-liability perspective in operation. This perspective implies a reality of some sort that all concerned should acknowledge and try to conform to. We are no more able unequivocally to announce what is in a dying person's interest than we are able fully to take responsibility for everything that happens as people die. Acknowledging the fallibility of one's own judgments creates space to resolve bitter disagreements. No one needs to despair that there is nothing that can be done. No one can take the viewpoint of someone who is "often wrong but never in doubt." Treating the patient's interest as trump, and the patient's own perception of that interest as dispositive until it is clearly self-destructive, puts family members, physicians, nurses, chaplains, and social workers in the position of consultants rather than authorities. Serious *inquiry*—rather than debate—about the patient's true interest is now required by the fact of universal fallibility.

Any serious religious perspective will underwrite this attitude. Shifting the moral center of gravity away from individuals and to God has the effect of smashing any claims that persons may have to superhuman powers or infallibility. We can compromise our understanding of what should be done and save our integrity, if we remember that spiritual or religious wholeness comes from a relation to God rather than from sticking to some pretty precarious judgments.[1]

Discerning Interest in the Midst of Disagreement

Families as well as professionals may struggle with disagreement. Assuming universal fallibility, exactly how are these disagreements to be dealt with? As many of the comments reported have shown, the professionals seek to build communities that focus on the patient's interest and in which patients are empowered. They are family communities of honesty, candor, and openness.

Empowering the patient is the first task. One chaplain who thinks of himself as an "attendant" described a patient who had had recurrent admissions to the hospital. "Her family was just denying. She had come into the hospital four or five times, and every time she would rally and go home. This time, she said, 'I'm not going to make it, and they're not ready.' I said, 'Well, how can we get them ready?' She said, 'Will you go talk to them? Will you?' And I said, 'I've *tried* to talk to them. They won't listen to me. The only person they'll listen to is you.' She said, 'Okay, bring them in, but only two at a time.' There were about three meetings. We took them in two at a time, and they would come out of there crying. I stayed with one of the groups. She said to them, 'Now I am *dying*.' They said, 'Oh, no. You've done well every time. Surely you'll recover.' 'No,' she said. 'I know I'm dying. My body tells me I'm dying. You've got to get ready.' She did it. She did it. She knew the time was getting right to make that shift. And she just needed some help to figure out what to do. When we finally devised a plan she was able to follow through with it. I just helped her implement the plan." Obviously these conversations were painful for all concerned, but both patient and chaplain realized that in this case true community was impossible in the face of denial.

As in this story, patients and family are also encouraged to speak for themselves when they are upset with forms of care that physicians or nurses are providing. "One of my mistakes early in my career was thinking that advocacy meant going to the doctor or nurse who was the source of the patient's or family's complaint and talking with them. I [concluded over the years] that was really kind of cheating the family. So basically my tack now is to say, 'I think you should take your concerns directly to the source. I'll support you in that in whatever way possible. And if that means making a fuss, then you make a fuss.' And on a few occasions, I've gotten in trouble. But that's a price I'm willing to pay." Without candor, authentic caring community is not possible.

Sometimes, however, things are more complicated. The exact source of disagreement and tension may not be obvious. "I view my role as trying to decipher, trying to get down to the bottom line of why there's a disagreement and what the bottom line is," says one social worker. "Whether it's a miscommunication or whatever that is. But my role would be to facilitate the patient's desires. The patient is my client, so to speak; my job is to make sure that that patient's able to do what they want, provided that that's safe. If it's huge, if it gets way blown out of proportion, a lot of times we can talk to people one-on-one and talk to the whole family and try and sort things out and usually come up with a compromise or work something out. Or it's a miscommunication issue many times, too."

The key step in this process of deciphering or being an attendant is listening. Not prying, but taking the time to listen. I asked a chaplain if he wasn't sometimes eager to learn more of a story than was volunteered. He replied: "If you sit down, shut up and listen long enough, people will tell you more than you ever wanted to know. And it's more important for this family to be able to tell their story as time evolves. Because if you pry like a policeman or a fireman, someone who is trying to get facts and figures, what you're going to do is jeopardize the grief process taking its own natural course. And you're probably going to tick this family off royally, because you don't want to ever come across as someone who's looking for the sensational details, but someone who is willing to sit and listen to them just be. A normal griever will go over and over and over everything that happened. A lot of these details I would not have if they had not shared them. And they needed to share them. And if you look like you're going to sit there and listen to them and be an active listener, rather than someone who is looking at their watch or fumbling with their keys or trying to figure out what the next page is coming in, people will tell you more than you ever really believed they ever would."

Listening is an end in itself; in addition, it can be a first step in enabling reconciliation and helpful decision making. Asked how he handles disagreements, another chaplain reported, "We attempt to approach [them] by listening. Realizing that what is happening is grief. And sometimes it will be a clear situation where the person has said, 'I don't want to be on life support.' Maybe you have got a spouse and three children who say, 'Yeah, I have heard Dad say that.' But here's this other son or this other daughter who just can't buy it. So you hope to spend some time simply listening. Not so much telling, but listening. And you hope you can help this person through whatever that is. If it is some regret that they have, some relationship that needs to be mended, some forgiveness, and some reconciliation. Sometimes it's some religious thing. You know, people maybe that are from the more conservative or fundamentalist end of the spectrum. If Dad hasn't been saved, they don't want to withdraw life support until Dad gets saved. Or sometimes it's things that are hard to get a handle on. They'll never be resolved. But I think the most we can do is to listen and see if there is some, like one log that is keeping this log jam from breaking free, and see if we can't facilitate that."

Practically speaking, how does this listening-based reconciliation strategy work? A first step is identification of someone with authority in the family. As a nurse put it, "I see my role as a mediator. And that happens a lot, believe it or not. What we try to do in that situation is try to pinpoint who is the closest relative. Sometimes we get *your* children and *our* children and *their* children, and it just seems to be a big conflict. So what we try to do is have one spokesperson with that situation, especially if it's a conflict, with us not giving everybody information. And we'll say, 'Okay, David is going to be the spokesperson here, and I'm going to tell David everything. You need to call him.'" Mediation or reconciliation does not start from scratch but begins with the actual relations that exist among people.

Recognizing the importance of these interactions can lead to constructive action, as in this chaplain's story. "What has worked best is if I can identify a spokesperson for the family. If I can get that family member off to the side and then ask, 'What do you think is going through your dad's mind right now? What does he say to you?' They may say 'Well, he doesn't say much to us.' So I will pursue that and then ask them, 'What do you think he might be thinking?' 'Well, I don't know.' 'How would you feel about asking him that? How would you feel about just saying, Dad, what would you like to talk about with us? About what's happening now?' And sometimes that works. It doesn't always work; sometimes it doesn't work that day. Maybe two or three conversations later, that conversation will come about within the family."

If appeals to family leadership don't work, meetings of all concerned may have to be held. Another chaplain reports that he tries to be a "conciliating factor." He goes on, "One of the methods I often use is asking patient care conferences to be called. That's probably the most used tactic I have. A patient care conference [entails] inviting as many family members as can come and as many physicians [as] are involved in that case that can be there, plus support for the [family], like child and social workers and others who are involved in the case to sit around the table, talk about what's going on medically, and hopefully come to some kind of consensus about what's going on. If not a consensus, [at least] so that everybody there knows where everybody else is coming from. Rather than getting it in bits and pieces or hearing one doctor say one thing and another doctor say another thing. And those have usually worked out well. Well enough that we've had probably few cases that come to the ethics committee, because the patient care conferences have seemed to work out the differences fairly well."

Others have had less success with this technique. Destructive family dynamics are not easily overcome. "A lot of times patients don't care if their doctor is mad at them. I mean, that's not as big a deal. They care a lot if their mom's mad at them. A lot of times, patients just don't even want that conflict. And they'll say, 'I really don't want to be on a ventilator, but if that's what my mom wants, I'll do it.' That leaves me wondering 'Okay, what do you want me to do here?' You can try and bring everybody together and talk about that. But then a lot of times, the patient won't speak up. And so they think, 'Oh, this nurse! This nurse is making trouble.' So I don't know, how do you handle conflict with families? I don't know. I'm not very good at it."

The intractable issues then may be resolved through a kind of diplomatic casuistry, trying to attain the least problematic outcome for the patient. One physician reported on such a situation. "This is a young, thirty-four-year-old man dying of brain cancer, and he's sort of been around the country seeking different treatments. And he's tied into an oncologist at X

University who he relates to well. And obviously he's gotten the physician very involved and he's still involved although he's a thousand miles away. And the physician talks to him practically every other day or [to] the family. And they still want to do IV therapy and various things that first struck me as inappropriate. But in looking at it from a different perspective, the family is very tied into his advice and his approach. And I thought it was wiser to go ahead and agree to what he wants to do, with just giving the family some caveats that we do have to be sure that IV fluids don't make him *more* uncomfortable, and if at some point we feel that maybe this is not the thing to do, to continue, then let's talk about it again and rethink it. I think it would probably not be very helpful to destroy that kind of relationship or to jump in the middle of this and say, 'What you're doing is wrong.' They've got a terrible amount of pain to deal with already. I think interjecting my opinions and insisting that you have to do it my way would not be the thing to do."

These professionals are very clear that they don't have privileged knowledge about what "God's will" for a particular patient may be. They are committed to various collegial processes through which caring persons can make their best guesses about what is really in the patient's interest. Epistemic modesty is entailed. The ideal conclusion will be one that is in the patient's interest and that concerned parties can live with. Groping for those conclusions takes time and requires a special form of community.

Engagement and Care Drive One into Community

But why remain in this world of disagreement; why not simply withdraw from the conflict? This brings us to the second perspective on the world that may be used in coping with the meaninglessness of death—a commitment to engagement with people in trouble, seeking meaning in helping them. I described some possible theological roots of such a perspective in the third chapter, noting that the people we talked to live it rather than articulating it. Thus what follows is my explanation of what they do, rather than one they offered themselves.

The fact is that many of these professionals stick with patients not only in the face of tragedy but when the patients are hard to tolerate. One chaplain reported "I walk into a patient's room, and [introduce myself and say] 'I just wanted to stop and meet you.' [One unforgettable patient said] 'Chaplain. I don't need a damn chaplain.' I said, 'Obviously there is some problem. So let me say I can be just your friend while you're here.' He said, 'Well, I don't know about that.' And I said, 'Well, would you mind if I just stop in and say hello from time to time?' And he said, 'Maybe that would be okay.' That's all that was said the first day. And the next day I just stopped in and said, 'How are you doing?' He said, 'I'm doing okay.' Next day, third day, fourth day, you know, I'm just doing this every day. I'm just stopping in to say hello. The next day he's getting ready to go home. He said, 'Chaplain, why don't you come on in here? You've been faithful to what you said you would do. You stopped in and said hello. You really deserve to know what's happened to me.' And I said, 'Well, I figured there was something, and I kind of hoped you would tell me.' He said, 'Last year I was very active in [a] church, and the [minister] ran off with my wife; I have not had any use for clergy since then. You don't deserve the kind of treatment I've given you. Thanks for being faithful to come and see me.' That's basically all that transpired."

Religion generally may be rejected; so may the particular color of religion in which the chaplain comes clothed. "I can't think of many situations where I've been turned down. Of course, everybody experiences that sometime or other in their professional career, where they just don't make contact. Most chaplains have been kicked out of a room at one time or the other. And that has happened to me. It was a terrible situation, where a young girl had a brain tumor, and she died. We were members of the same tradition, but they [were much more conservative] and probably didn't like me too much. At first, I had a good relationship with the mother, but the father was particularly the dominant person. And eventually he didn't want to have too much to do with me. Even their own [clergyman] was a little confused by what they were doing. And yet this is what families do in a tragic, terrible situation. [Other bad things happened to them] and I went in, but I don't think I was appreciated too much." Presence can be offered, but there is no guarantee of its acceptance.

Making this offering without being coercive or intrusive is a first challenge these reflective nurses and chaplains face. A second is how to sustain themselves when their work is clearly not appreciated. One remarkable nurse was asked if her work ever challenged her religious beliefs. We expected a philosophical response about the goodness or justice of God. Instead she said, "Oh, my goodness, yes. Of just the simple things of trying when you're doing your best to please families and patients and whatever, and then they lash out at you or say you're incompetent or believe you don't have the patient's best interest at heart. That hurts. And then you want to lash out back. And that is certainly not the right attitude, either. And then you have to start backing off. Our social service folks have really been a great help to us. They say, 'Now wait a minute. Think about this. Are they lashing out at you, or are they lashing out because they are angry about dying?' So you have to put everything in perspective and regroup then and go back and think about what you're doing."

Rejection presented this nurse not with an intellectual crisis, but with a moral test. Could she be the kind of person she thought her religion required her to be when facing a complete lack of appreciation? Her answer was to appreciate the help she was given and to pace herself. "I am on sabbatical from hospice right now. For a while I was taking calls for them and worked about six times a month on call. But I had to take a sabbatical. One night, in the middle of the night, this wife called me, and she said, 'He won't take his pill.' And I gave her some ideas about how to get him to take it, and she said, 'No, I can't.' So I had to get up at 2:00 in the morning and go out and give that patient his pill. And he took it fine, [but] I got real angry with her. And I thought, 'Wait a minute here. If you're going to get angry, it's time to take a sabbatical.' So that's why. I'm going to go back."

These stories reveal just the visible tip of the iceberg of the dedicated care that these professionals offer. They clearly demonstrate the importance of creation of community among the caregivers. Supported dedication, including the possibility of "taking a sabbatical," is much easier to sustain than solitary dedication. Traditional or nontraditional religious or spiritual commitments push these professionals into situations in which they are expected, and want, to keep on giving. But that is no easy task. Community building in the caregiving setting is of remarkable religious and spiritual importance.

Fragments of Meaning and Fragmentary Communities

I have tried to show that the partial worldviews rooted in the religious or spiritual lives of these professionals contribute to creation of community in a couple of ways. First, they enable perspective on disagreement and make it possible to recognize the limited and fragmentary character of everyone's point of view. This makes constructive deliberation possible. Second, they drive the professionals to try to create or sustain community with patients and within patients' families. In fact, as we have seen, religion can be divisive. But it need not be; in fact it can provide crucial perspective and motivation. I do not contend that many, if any, of these professionals harmonize these two partial worldviews or spiritual perspectives in their own lives. They may or may not; my data provide no way of telling. Harmonization on a strictly intellectual or systematic level *might* be difficult. I am sure that these perspectives have some rooting in their lives and can provide a basis for serious conversation.

Community creation is a central part of what religion can contribute to care for the dying, but how can hospitals and churches assure that this and other contributions mentioned earlier really occur? I will take up that question in the conclusion.

Notes

1. This argument is an adaptation of one made by Martin Benjamin, *Splitting the Difference: Compromise and Integrity in Ethics* (Lawrence: University of Kansas Press, 1990).

CHAPTER SIX

~

Conclusion

To review the ground covered so far: I have claimed that the ethics of care for the dying will be improved if the role of religion in the minds and work of professionals is taken seriously. What do physicians, nurses, social workers, and chaplains think about the moral and religious issues in care for the dying? If we have a partial answer to that question, we may have something to build on as we try to help them improve that care. What have we learned?

First, we have learned that these professionals live with death, including many untimely and difficult deaths, on a daily basis. At least one of the persons we interviewed makes sense of this emotionally draining situation by making use of a very traditional theodicy: the suffering will be compensated for in a resurrected life. But for the vast majority of this cohort—Catholic, Protestant, Jewish, and spiritual—comprehensive schemes for explaining or justifying the evil in the world are fatuous. Such a scheme *may* have a role in a systematic theology, but its immediate personal relevance is minimal. Rather, these professionals make do with one of what we have been calling fragments of meaning. The first is the notion that God (whoever or whatever God may be), rather than the self, is in charge. Ultimate responsibility for whatever may happen lies beyond the self—in the hands of Fate or God, they might say; "Everything does not depend on me." This liberation from ultimate responsibility can be salvific for persons in roles in which their judgments, bad luck, or manner may greatly affect whether and how someone dies.

Second, many of the professionals find meaning by deeply engaging themselves with their patients. They don't have a conceptual answer as to how to find meaning in the face of suffering, but they have an existential answer: by dedicating themselves to improving the care of dying persons. In terms of Christian theology—the tradition which has had the greatest influence on our cohort—this is a highly Christological solution to the problem of finding meaning in suffering and death, for it amounts to a kind of *imitatio Christi*—acting as the Christ would have acted. The solution to an intellectual problem is not found through intellectual speculation but through living a life of a certain kind.

If we learned nothing else from the interviews, this simple lesson about meaning in the face of suffering would be invaluable, for it suggests that these professionals don't need to turn to moralists or theologians in order to work out a way of life in the face of death and suffering. At any rate they don't need to turn to them for comprehensive solutions. If they have an intellectual need, it is to be listened to and taken seriously in their spiritual wonderings; to encounter clear conversation partners; to have space and time to work things out for themselves.

Our respondents' insights on suffering and death are reflected in their views on physician-assisted suicide. None of them really favors this controversial practice, but several of them think it may be appropriate as an act of individual con-scientious objection to a general rule in a few difficult situa-tions. They are torn between their recognition of their own and their colleagues' fallibility and finitude, recognition that professional power should know some limits, and a deep com-mitment to doing whatever they can to help relieve suffering. On the whole, they think that working for legalization of physician-assisted suicide is a misplaced reform strategy. It would be better, they think, to work at the issues that lead to the requests for physician-assisted suicide in the first place—to better inform the public about problems with end-of-life care and resources to deal with them, and to assure provision of adequate palliative care for all citizens.

Their convictions about these matters require development of policies that will allow provision of the widest possible menu of non-murderous palliative care strategies at the end of life. This means recognizing that some actions that may be "causes" of death are not morally culpable acts of murder. Caregivers should avoid scrupulous tendencies to blame them-selves for everything, thus concluding that every act that leads to death amounts to unjustified killing. Nor should they con-clude that, since killing is OK, the only issue is counting the cost to all concerned. What's needed is a sensible and secular reworking of the rule of double effect.

But this reworking calls for the creation of serious communi-ties of conversation in hospitals, nursing homes, clinics, and other settings where end-of-life care is provided. The really diffi-cult cases call for conversation and community support rather than clandestine "conscientious objection." These arguments thus imply that anything that can be done to create honest com-munities in care settings will pay rich dividends in improvements in care for the dying. The key people want to do better; they need ways of learning from and supporting each other.

Religion, so often a source of division, can greatly contribute to the creation of community in many ways. The stress on the sovereignty of God has the effect of reminding persons that their own perspectives and judgments are finite and contingent. Thus thoughtful persons are liberated to discuss options they might not have considered or to support choices they might not originally have made without feeling that they are selling out. They aren't selling out because their ultimate loyalty is to a Higher Power or God rather than to an ideology. Compromise and learning replace the moral absolutism that comes with attempts completely to depend on oneself. Moreover, religion motivates persons to enter stressful workplace communities and to stick it out despite the psychological costs. The religious perspectives we have surveyed suggest that the patient, as a person who is living out the last days of his or her life, should be the moral fulcrum as disputes inevitably arise within families, within the mind of the patient, and between caregivers and families. There is no universal theological rule for dispute resolution, but religiously or spiritually serious persons should be particularly eager to work out strategies for aiding in reconciliation.

What Should Be Done?

I think I have shown that religious communities are the sort of groups that should be engaged with the social problem of dying in the United States, and that they could have some helpful, fresh, and distinctive things to contribute. Specifically what does that entail?

First, religious communities should provide moral and spiritual support to their members who are involved with care for the dying. This means, first, listening to them and learning what issues are on their minds, what conclusions they have come to, and what recommendations they might make for worship and education. The willingness of our respondents to talk, to share their uncertainties, and to speak critically about both religious and health care institutions and personnel was truly remarkable. Many conversations were accompanied by tears (from interviewee and interviewer). Simply providing the opportunity to talk, taking the moral and spiritual lives of these professionals seriously, renders an important pastoral service. Health professionals should expect, even demand, that religious communities provide them with this form of ministry.

Moreover, many—although not all—of the persons we spoke to would welcome the chance to share their ideas and experiences with a larger group of people. To be sure, this book attempts to do some of that, albeit it in a filtered and imperfect way. But thoughtful and religiously reflective professionals are a remarkable and largely untapped resource for local or regional educational programs. They can't be programmed. They won't stay with any official script. But they will bring a note of honesty to congregational discussion of care for the dying and they will be listened to, even when they are disagreed with.

This brings us to the second main thing that religious communities should do, and that is engage in vital education programs dealing with aging, death, and care for the dying. I have tried to suggest some topics for those programs in the course of this book. They include ways of coping with suffering and death; moral limits on what we should do in providing each other with loving care; candid discussions of life after death; and an imperative to serve as agents of reconciliation. But this only scratches the surface. Other obvious topics include practical legal issues such as the role of various advance directives, reflection on the question of setting limits on one's own striving to stay alive, and the values and virtues of aging.

If these congregational programs are effective, they will stimulate conversations among family and close friends. The importance of these conversations, of listening to family members and making one's wishes known, can scarcely be exaggerated. Persons fortunate enough to be able to expect continuity of care between their primary care physician and the place where they can expect to spend their last days should be sure that the physician and his or her associates are "in the loop" of these conversations. Everyone should take steps to assure that all anticipated players in decision making at the end of life understand the values and vision that will guide treatment decisions, even if they do not agree with them. Religious congregations themselves cannot assure that these serious conversations will occur, but they can provide the stimulus for them, information that will be helpful in them, and help in setting a constructive tone for them.

Initiating this kind of programming may not absolutely require clergy initiative, but clergy indifference would certainly make it difficult to get it started or conduct it well. Clergy, as the rest of us, are often bewildered by the overwhelming grief and spiritual pain that death may entail. They don't have, and shouldn't have, easy answers. They should, however, receive support as they initiate discussion in uncharted territory. In preparation they need some settings in which they can read and reflect and talk together about ways of providing the support and educational programs that their congregations need. They need encouragement to make dealing with death a vital part of their ministries, from pulpit to outreach to education. Funding is needed to support such seminars for clergy, and they will be most effective if laypersons who are physicians and nurses are also present. There's a place for both denomination-specific and interfaith programs.

However, there is an even more distinctly religious line of approach to issues of care for the dying. It relates to worship and devotion.

Rituals

A final dimension of religious initiative should be attention to ritual. Community and ritual are intrinsically yoked concepts. Whatever the rituals be—those of reading from scripture, liturgical drama, or the confession of sins—religious communities grasp that they are central to their communities' health. It's hard to sustain a vital religious community if worship is boring, unintelligible, or vapid. Good ritual has at least two characteristics: it is meaningful, and to some degree it is habitual. Ritual is precisely not something that one continuously improvises. It has constant elements; it has a certain degree of predictability; it is reliable. Anyone who is at all attuned to religion should appreciate the importance of ritual.

We often depict these characteristics of ritual in a critical vein. We say that some political or economic statement or act was "just pure ritual," by which we mean inauthentic or insincere. In fact families, workplaces, and educational institutions are sustained by rituals: of athletic contests or eating together, of staff meetings, lunch conversations, and daily greetings; of matriculation, graduation, and special recognition. At its best, ritual is a social habit that marks important transitions in our lives and loves. Ritual helps us get through difficult points; it relates to routine and habit—essential aspects of life that we too often take for granted.

Groups that are involved in care for the dying need ritual debriefings, moments of silence, and confessions as part of their professional routine. These rituals need not be religious in any traditional sense; they should simply help to sustain the diverse pieties of persons trying to cope with recurrent and intense encounters with death. The expectation of these ritual moments is essential to sanity; their provision should be habitual.

Good ritual requires more than regularity; it requires some allocation of space and time. Consider the remarks of a nurse describing some of her conflicts over end-of-life care: "Sometimes I was angry about the whole issue of physicians not being honest with their patients. That was really hard for me to deal with. And, you know, them saying, 'You can't talk to her about dying, because I haven't had the discussion with her yet.' 'Well, when are you going to have the discussion, then? It's time to do it.' And that was hard. Not that it was scary. It just made me mad. I don't think I was ever scared, once I got past that first patient who died. I had one situation where the physician was treating the patient very aggressively. And I thought it was time to back off. And we actually went into a conference room, and we had a fight. I mean, a yelling fight about what was ethical and not ethical, and why was he doing this? And if this was for his research, that was not a good enough reason. And we went round and round and round about that. But he was the rare physician who was willing to go into a conference room with you and do that. Not that I got my way in the end, because I didn't. But he listened. Most of them, you can't get that much of their time. You know, they don't want to talk about it. They're busy."

Translating this statement into my jargon, this nurse is suggesting that space and time need to be carved out for these conversations. They should not occur in the corridor, as many of them do; they should not be completely ad hoc, as she suggests they usually are. They are integral parts of the life of the caregiving community, and resources of space and time must be committed to make them possible. Providing resources for the humane side of care for the dying, for regular conversations about things that matter desperately, is something that matters as much as provision of adequate technological resources.

Of course, there is also an important place for traditional religious rituals. These may be moments of silence, anointing, prayer, or eucharist. The traditional rituals signal that the community of the hospital or hospice or deathbed is only one context in which a dying or dead person is seen. Traditional ritual casts events onto a larger stage or context; in that they are invaluable. However, they need to be effective, clear, and appropriate to new realities. For example, traditional rituals for respirator disconnection or for a moment at which feeding tubes are disconnected could be, and in some cases have been, developed.[1]

There is a danger of misplaced ritual—of assuming, for example, that every Jew will want to see the rabbi or that every Catholic desires anointing. Even worse, there is also a danger of imposing rituals from traditions foreign or uncongenial to the tradition in which a patient has oriented his life. The professionals in this study, who some might think are peculiarly prone to making such a mistake because of their interest in religion or spirituality, in fact clearly view such an error as a terrible one, as we saw in chapters 2 and 5. Everything for them hangs on the particularity of the patient. Reflectiveness about the spiritual components of care leads to sensitivity about religion.

But the poverty of traditional ritual support for workers in the health professions is, at least, unfortunate. The professionals we spoke to who do regularly attend corporate worship do not report getting much support from it. This is a sad commentary, for it seems natural to think that worship would mesh with the worries and disappointments of persons who care for the dying. The mesh might be conceptual—through preaching that directly addresses issues raised by human mortality and disability. Or it might come in more indirect ways in the form of hymnody and liturgical actions that touch the soul. If religious worship fails to reach the people in our sample on some level, it is hard to see how it can claim to be about fundamental or basic matters of human life and destiny.

Meanwhile, this study suggests some important steps that health care institutions themselves can take to improve care for the dying. Essentially they need to make room for spiritual care through provision of time and space for conversation, inquiry, and mutual support. One obvious step in the right direction is to assure that a hospital's chaplain staff is large and competent enough to adequately discern where improvement is needed and skilled enough to assist other care providers in establishing practices and procedures of support. It should be clear that the chaplains' charge includes attention to the spiritual needs of physicians and nurses.

Moreover, hospitals, hospices, and nursing homes will find their work made much easier if they are dealing with populations who have given thought to end-of-life care for themselves and their loved ones. The health care institutions can do some public education themselves, but perhaps more importantly they can help local or regional religious leaders and institutions to do it well. This may mean sponsoring conferences or ongoing seminars of local religious leaders or providing speakers to visit adult education classes of local congregations.

Predictable Objections

I have tried to illustrate how religious institutions and traditions, Christianity in particular, can assist in efforts to improve the care of the dying in the United States. Speaking very broadly, they can perform that assistance through clearly defending ideas that are at the core of their existence. They can provide comfort and assistance to professionals who are looking for ways to sustain themselves as caregivers, and they can convincingly advocate the creation of some characteristics of workplace community, notably the ritual structures and traditions that make those communities more humane, as well as the freedom for traditional ritual.

Someone is sure to respond with something like this: I don't care about religion and neither do most of the people I know. Our major awareness of religion in the caregiving setting is when it becomes a problem, an impediment to the provision of palliative care or therapy. We're better off not mucking around with it. Religious foibles are anachronistic in an age of scientific medicine. Serious care for the dying is well beyond the kinds of issues you are raising.

I want to respond to this important criticism on several levels.

First, although improvements in care for the dying have occurred in the past quarter century or more, they are not pervasive, uniformly accessible, or even secure. These reforms have progressed largely with religious communities on the sidelines. But many Americans think of themselves as religious or spiritual. Strictly in terms of cultural politics, doesn't it make sense to try to build a vital connection to religious communities to attempt to strengthen the reform effort?

Second, I hold no brief for the view that Christianity or even religious traditions in general are *necessary* in order to provide the kind of attention to suffering, the moral guidelines for care for the dying, or the creation of workplace community that is needed today. Secular analogues can be created; much argument about human destiny, morality, and life together can and should proceed without any explicitly religious referent. But why insist on this purge in a pluralistic society? When actual people's lives are shaped by traditions, it makes sense to try to integrate the most vital and insightful portions of those traditions into our public discussion of care for the dying. Religious hegemony should never be insisted on—or allowed. But religious participation is an essential component of our public conversation.

Third, the point in my argument where the dangers of religious involvement are most likely to prove objectionable is in opposition to physician-assisted suicide. For example, Ronald Dworkin argues in *Life's Dominion* that the issue in physician-assisted death (and abortion) is the sacredness of life.[2] But part of the American polity, he continues, is resistance to the idea of an establishment of religion, or canonizing anyone's idea of what is sacred. Moreover, Americans disagree about the implications of seeing death choices as pertaining to the sacred. Many deny that "sacredness" is involved. Because our constitution guarantees us freedom of religion, we should have full freedom of individual choice at the end of life, including the choice of physician-assisted suicide.

However, it takes only a little reflection to see that there must be some moral restrictions on freedom of religious exercise. And the paradigmatic cases come with reference to killing. If someone defends himself against a charge of killing his wife on the grounds that his religion requires stoning her to death, we will either laugh him out of court or consider a defense of insanity. The real question is not whether freedom of conscientious action can be limited at all, but what the fair grounds for those limits on liberty are.

I contend that the best grounds for restriction of freedom are not to be found in abstract logic but in the life and sensibilities of citizens themselves. Nor am I alone in holding to this view. As Michael Walzer argues, the most powerful forms of social or political argument arise from commitments that a community really shares; he calls this the practice of "connected criticism."[3] There is a role for a critic who uses abstract or universal values, who is armed perhaps only with logic, but that role is limited. We listen to people who appeal to values we hold. Resistance to—at best uncertainty about—acts that are unequivocally lethal is such a value. Resistance to legalization of physician-assisted suicide is connected to a broad range of religious and spiritual sensibilities in our culture, sensibilities that the persons we interviewed all share.

Fortunately, resistance to physician-assisted suicide is not the only social imperative they feel that is essential. Others include respect for individual choice and a duty to relieve suffering. As I go beyond the formulations of the interviewees on physician-assisted suicide, I have tried my best to work out a position on the issue that acknowledges our cultural perplexity and dilemma.

Finally, this broadside against support for the role of religion in discussion of care for the dying may imply that I am not neutral among religious perspectives. To take simply Christianity, the main tradition with which I have been concerned, the versions of theodicy, or morality, or community creation that I defend are certainly contested terrain among Christians. There is no single Christian view of any of these topics, and if there were it's unclear that my version would be it.

On one level I plead guilty to this charge. That is, I concede that my theology—such as it is—is fragmentary and highly vulnerable to criticism. I can speak only for myself, however much I have tried to root my ideas in the conversations that provide so much of the substance of this book. To me, however, it is unclear that we have a good alternative to the venture I have undertaken. If we are seriously to deliberate about the role of religion in care for the dying, we have to face the fact that the religious "side" of the argument has something to learn as well as something to teach.

Michael Perry makes this point about deliberation very well.[4] He distinguishes among purposes for which we may engage in conversation about social issues. As he notes, I may simply mean to "witness" or testify to my own conviction. Valuable as that is, it need persuade no one. Second, I may try to persuade you to come around to my point of view—a debater's move in which I use any argument that I think may have weight with you, whether I take it seriously myself or not. Or, I may offer a justification of a conclusion based on reasons you and I both take seriously. This is a major step beyond the first two options, because it assumes a kind of equality with one's conversation partner, not the certainty that one is correct.

But beyond these important forms of social discussion (each of which may have its place) lies *deliberation*, in which a speaker acknowledges his or her fallibility and finitude and the fact that there is something here to learn. Deliberation calls for the courage to admit fallibility—that one has something to learn, as well as something to say. I've tried to suggest what religious communities might say, the kinds of things they might want to talk about, and the kinds of responsibilities they could take on. But those proposals are rooted in listening and learning. All theologies are not created equal in these contexts, and there is no avoiding an attempt at a fair-minded assessment of theological proposals. Unwillingness to deliberate reflects an unwillingness fully to engage with one's conversation partners and a betrayal of the sovereignty of God.

The Morals of This Story

1. Religious communities should be very proactive in seeking out, listening to, and supporting persons involved in care for the dying.
2. Religious leaders should be comfortable and not defensive in their conversations about care for the dying.

Stressing the sovereignty of God and the value of dedicated service are natural themes to sound.

3. When the moral question of physician-assisted suicide comes up, we should urge broadening the issue and support every form of comfort provision and humane care that can honestly be described as in the patient's interest.

4. Religious communities should invest time and treasure in education programs about end-of-life care for clergy, health care professionals, and for all members of congregations. These must be honest, well-informed, and clear. They need not be depressing. To the contrary, they will buoy spirits.

5. Institutions in which people die must provide time, space, and conditions of employment so as to ensure the creation of community among health care providers. This will entail the creation of secular rituals on wards or other units; it should also allow space for more traditional rituals with patients or health care providers as and when such may be desired. Religious communities should insist on any reforms that may be necessary to make these things possible.

This is in no way an impossible menu to try to offer. Nor should it be highly controversial. It specifies something of indisputable importance that religious communities should make one of their very highest priorities. I've tried to explain why. It will be my good luck if some readers of this book are encouraged in their work for this end. Dying is too tough for religious communities to fail to help us with it.

Notes

1. For example, see Cynthia Cohen et al., *Faithful Living, Faithful Dying: Anglican Reflections on End of Life Care* (Harrisburg, Penn.: Morehouse Publishing, 2000).

2. Ronald Dworkin, *Life's Dominion: An Argument over Abortion, Euthanasia, and Individual Freedom* (New York: Alfred A. Knopf, Inc., 1993).

3. Michael Walzer, *Interpretation and Social Criticism* (Cambridge, Mass.: Harvard University Press, 1987).

4. Michael Perry, *Love and Power: The Role of Religion and Morality in American Politics* (New York: Oxford University Press, 1991).

~

Appendix

Interview Questions for Physicians

1. How did you come to be practicing this medical specialty?
2. What sorts of death are the hardest for you to deal with? Please tell me about one or two patients whose deaths you remember well. Is it relevant to distinguish among acute death, death from violence, death after chronic illness?
3. What worries you about caring for dying patients? What scares you? Do you feel prepared to care for the dying?
4. What rules or rules of thumb guide you in making decisions about treatment for dying patients? (Probe: Patient preferences? Family wishes? Preservation of life? Minimizing suffering? Legal standards? Reimbursement policies? Advance directives?)
5. Do you think your views about care for the dying are typical of physicians you work with? Or are you different? If so, in what way?

6. How do your views about care for the dying (or those of other physicians) compare with those of nurses or clergy? What other professionals, besides physicians, is it important to consult?

7. Do you discuss death with anyone? (Probe: Other physicians? Nurses? Chaplains? Other clergy? Family?)

8. What do we do well in care for the dying? What could we do better?

9. What is the worst thing a physician can do in caring for a dying patient? How much of this goes on? Is it or should it be grounds for professional discipline?

10. What are the most common mistakes made by physicians? What do they usually do well?

11. What do dying patients/families expect from health care providers? Are their expectations reasonable?

12. Do you support physician-assisted suicide and/or euthanasia for those with terminal or irreversibly debilitative illness?

13. Have you ever encountered a situation in which your views about care for the dying conflict with patients' expectations or family preferences? How have you handled those situations?

14. What factors influence your present views about care for the dying? Are your views influenced by your peers? Your teachers? A religious community?

15. How have you encountered death in your personal life? Have those experiences affected your professional practice in any way?

16. How often do you think about your own and others' mortality? Have you noticed a difference since you began practicing medicine?

17. How has working with dying patients affected your personal views about your own death or the death of a family member or close friend?

18. Were you raised in a religious tradition? Does religious belief play a role in your life? If so, what? Do you think of yourself as a religious person? What, if any, of your religious beliefs are most relevant to your work in care for the dying?
19. Does your work challenge your religious beliefs?
20. How do you care for dying patients whose beliefs differ from your own? Do the beliefs of people from different cultures affect you in different ways?
21. Do your religious beliefs help in your work? How?
22. Where do you get support? (Probe: Family? Peers? Religious community?)
23. Would you advise one of your children to go to medical school? Are the kinds of issues we have been discussing relevant to the decision?
24. Are there particular values bearing on care for the dying that you'd especially like to pass on? What are they?
25. Do you read patients' obituaries? What do you look for?
26. Do you attend patients' visitations or funerals? If so, how do you decide which ones to attend?
27. Do you write, call, or contact surviving family members after a patient's death?
28. What have I left out? What would you like to add?

Interview Questions for Nurses

1. What is your current job title? How did you come to be practicing this nursing specialty?
2. What sorts of death are the hardest for you to deal with? Please tell me about one or two patients whose deaths you remember well. Is it relevant to distinguish among acute death, death from violence, death after chronic illness?

3. What worries you about caring for dying patients? What scares you? Do you feel prepared to care for the dying?

4. Do you think your views about care for the dying are typical of nurses you work with? Or are you different? If so, in what way?

5. How do your views on care for the dying (or those of other nurses) compare with those of physicians or clergy? What other professionals, besides nurses, is it important to consult?

6. Do you discuss death with anyone? (Probe: Physicians? Nurses? Chaplains? Other clergy? Family?)

7. What do we do well in care for the dying? What could we do better?

8. What are the most common mistakes made by physicians? What do they usually do well?

9. What is the worst thing a nurse can do in caring for a dying patient? How much of this goes on? Is it or should it be grounds for professional discipline?

10. What do dying patients/families expect from health care providers? Are their expectations reasonable?

11. Do you support physician-assisted suicide and/or euthanasia for those with terminal or irreversibly debilitative illness?

12. Have you ever encountered a situation in which your views about care for the dying conflict with patients' expectations or family preferences? How have you handled those situations?

13. How do you define your role when conflict occurs within the family or between the patient/family and caregivers?

14. What factors influence your present views about care for the dying? Are your views influenced by your peers? Your teachers? A religious community?

15. Have you encountered death in your personal life? Have those experiences affected your professional practice in any way?

16. How has working with dying patients affected your personal views about your own death or the death of a family member or close friend?

17. How often do you think about your own and others' mortality? Have you noticed a difference since you began your nursing career?

18. Were you raised in a religious tradition? Does religious belief play a role in your life? If so, what? Do you think of yourself as a religious person? What, if any, of your religious beliefs are most relevant to your work in care for the dying?

19. Do your religious beliefs help in your work? How?

20. Does your work challenge your religious beliefs?

21. How do you care for dying patients whose beliefs differ from your own? Do the beliefs of people from different cultures affect you in different ways?

22. Where do you get support? (Probe: Family? Peers? Religious community?)

23. Would you advise one of your children to go to nursing school? Are the kinds of issues we have been discussing relevant to the decision?

24. Are there particular values bearing on care for the dying that you'd especially like to pass on to young nurses? What are they?

25. Do you read patients' obituaries? What do you look for?

26. Do you attend patients' visitations or funerals? If so, how do you decide which ones to attend?

27. Do you write, call, or contact surviving family members after a patient's death?

28. What have I left out? What would you like to add?

Interview Questions for Chaplains

1. Why did you enter the ministry? How did you come to exercise this particular form of ministry?
2. Please tell me about one or two patients whose deaths you remember well. Why are those deaths memorable? Is it relevant to distinguish among acute death, death from violence, death after chronic illness?
3. What worries you about caring for dying patients? What scares you? Do you feel prepared to care for the dying?
4. Do you think your views about care for the dying are typical of clergy you work with? Or are you different? If so, in what way?
5. How do your views on care for the dying (or those of other clergy) compare with those of physicians or nurses?
6. Do you discuss death with anyone? (Probe: Physicians? Nurses? Chaplains? Other clergy? Family?)
7. What do we do well in care for the dying? What could we do better?
8. What is the worst thing a chaplain can do in caring for a dying patient? How much of this goes on? Is it or should it be grounds for professional discipline?
9. What are the most common mistakes made by chaplains? What do they usually do well?
10. What do dying patients/families expect from health care providers? Are their expectations reasonable?
11. Do you support physician-assisted suicide and/or euthanasia for those with terminal or irreversibly debilitative illness?
12. Have you ever encountered a situation in which your views about care for the dying conflict with patients' expectations or family preferences? How have you handled those situations? Do the beliefs of people from different cultures affect you in different ways?

13. How do you define your role when conflict occurs within the family or between the patient/family and caregivers?
14. What factors have formed your present views about care for the dying? Are your views influenced by your peers? Your teachers? A religious community?
15. How have you encountered death in your personal life? Have those experiences affected your professional practice in any way?
16. How often do you think about your own and others' mortality? Have you noticed a difference since you became a chaplain?
17. How has working with dying patients affected your personal views about your own death or the death of a family member or close friend?
18. Does your work challenge your religious beliefs?
19. Do your religious beliefs help in your work? How? In different ways?
20. Where do you get support? (Probe: Family? Peers? Religious community?)
21. Would you advise one of your children to go to seminary? Are the kinds of issues we have been discussing relevant to that decision? If your child was considering ministry, would you recommend the chaplaincy?
22. Are there particular values bearing on care for the dying that you'd especially like to pass on? What are they?
23. Do you read patients' obituaries? What do you look for?
24. Do you attend patients' visitations or funerals? If so, how do you decide which ones to attend?
25. Do you write, call, or contact surviving family members after a patient's death?
26. What have I left out? What would you like to add?

Index

Adams, Marilyn McCord,
44–45
American Health Decisions, 2

Battin, Margaret Pabst, 70–71
bioethics: patient autonomy
movement in, 4–5;
professional dominance
issues, 4; on types of end-of-
life care, 63–82

Cassel, Christine, 76–77
centering prayer, 25
Chambliss, Daniel, 30
chaplains: on belief of afterlife,
59–62; dealing with
disagreements around dying,
84–106; dedication of,
103–4; diversity in ministries
of, 35–36; listening and

communicating skills of,
33–37, 55, 97–102; on
personal presence, 53,
54–59; role in congregations,
3–4; on role of God in
suffering and death, 41–42,
48, 88–95; spirituality in
work identity of, 6, 26, 28,
33–37, 111; views on
physician-assisted suicide,
64–81
Christianity/Christian tradition:
on crisis of suffering and
death, 1, 7; place in
improving the care of dying,
52–53, 108. *See also* religious
communities
communities: of caregivers,
83–106. *See also* religious
communities

conversation partners: interviews of, 11, 15–38, 123–29; professional spirituality of, 15, 26–37; traditional religion of, 15, 16–26

death: fear of, 1, 2, 72; as technological event, 1. *See also* dying/end-of-life
Death of Ivan Illych, The (Tolstoy), 56
Dworkin, Ronald, 118
dying/end-of-life: communities of caregivers in, 11, 83–106; coping with suffering in, 1, 10, 28; denial about, 90–93, 97–99; directed dying in, 70–71; disagreements and conflicts surrounding, 11, 84–106; families coping with, 31, 56, 84–85; impact of professional personal presence, 53–59, 72, 74–75; moral issues in care of, 9–12; palliative and pain-control measures for, 28, 72–74, 109; patient care conferences during, 100–102; patient's interests and preferences with, 70–71, 88–102; physical and biological facts of, 56, 61, 73–74; public education about, 111–12, 116, 121; role of God in, 39–62, 88–95; sacredness in, 118–19; as spiritually demanding work, 6, 7, 111; types and forms of

care for, 63–82; values and issues with, 2, 6, 7, 111. *See also* physician-assisted suicide (PAS)

Eliot, T. S., 46–47
euthanasia. *See* physician-assisted suicide (PAS)

"Generalization of Expertise" (Veatch), 4

health care professionals: dedication in care of dying, 102–5; ritual support in communities of, 113–16; spirituality of, 15, 26–37, 111; traditional religion of, 15, 16–26. *See also specific professionals*
health care systems, end-of-life care by, 2
health professionals: caregiver communities of, 81; patient support of, 58; perceptions and values of, 4–5; on personal presence of, 53–59; in religious communities, 3–4; on role of God in suffering and death, 39–62, 88–95; roles in end-of-life care, 3; spirituality of, 6, 111. *See also specific professionals*

Keating, Thomas, 25
Kevorkian, Jack, 67
Kushner, Harold, 50–51

Life's Dominion (Dworkin), 118

meditation, 25
Mehlman, Max, 66
Mohrmann, Margaret, 44, 54
Moltmann, Jurgen, 52
moral conversation, 8, 11

nurses: on belief of afterlife,
59–62; challenges in
profession of, 30–32; dealing
with disagreements around
dying, 84–106; dedication in
care of dying, 103–5;
listening and communicating
skills of, 30–32, 97–102, 114;
on personal presence of,
53–59; in religious
communities, 3–4; on role of
God in suffering and death,
40–41, 46, 88–95; spirituality
in work identity of, 6, 26, 28,
30–32, 34, 35, 37, 111;
traditional religion of, 15, 19,
24, 25; views on physician-
assisted suicide, 64–81

On the Edge of Being, 57

Patient as Person, The (Ramsey),
6
Perry, Michael, 120
physician-assisted suicide
(PAS): double effect of,
75–78, 109; general rules and
responsibility of, 67–69,
78–80; health professional

views of, 11, 36, 63, 64–69,
108–9, 118–19, 121;
legalization of, 63; medical
necessity or premature
choice of, 64, 66–67, 75;
religious and spiritual aspects
of, 69–82, 111
physicians: on belief of afterlife,
59–62; dealing with
disagreements around dying,
84–106; dedication in care of
dying, 103–5; listening and
communicating skills of,
29–30, 97–102, 114;
palliative care versus curing
skills of, 28–30; on personal
presence, 53–59; in religious
communities, 3–4; on role of
God in suffering and death,
40, 46, 50, 88–95; spirituality
in work identity of, 26,
27–30, 34, 37, 111;
traditional religion of, 15,
16–26; views on physician-
assisted suicide, 64–81

Ramsey, Paul, 6
reflective practice, 8–9
religious communities:
contributions to caregiver
communities, 83–106,
110–13; good ritual in,
113–16; health professional
memberships in, 3–4; roles in
end-of-life care, 2–3, 12,
107–21; traditional religion
of professionals in, 15, 16–26

retributivist theodicy, 9
rituals, in creating communities and support, 12, 113–16
Robert Wood Johnson Foundation, 2

social workers: dealing with disagreements around dying, 84–106; dedication in care of dying, 104–5; in religious communities, 3–4; on role of God in suffering and death, 47, 88–95; spirituality in work identity of, 6, 26, 111; traditional religion of, 15, 20–21; views on physician-assisted suicide, 69

spirituality: of end-of-life caregivers, 6, 15, 26–37, 111. *See also specific professionals*
suffering, coping with, 10–11
SUPPORT study, 30–31

Tolstoy, Leo, 56

Veatch, Robert M., 4
Verhey, Allen, 74

Walzer, Michael, 118
Weber, Max, 48
When Bad Things Happen to Good People (Kushner), 50–51
worship and devotion, ritual of, 113–16

~

About the Author

David H. Smith taught in the Department of Religious Studies at Indiana University–Bloomington for thirty-six years before his retirement in 2003. He has written on various topics in medical ethics; he also writes on moral issues associated with trying to help out, a side of his work that he likes to call "paved with good intentions."